WHERE
THE
SPIRITS
DWELL

ALSO BY
TOBIAS SCHNEEBAUM

Keep the River on Your Right
Wild Man

WHERE
THE
SPIRITS
DWELL

*An Odyssey in the
New Guinea Jungle*

Tobias Schneebaum

GROVE PRESS
New York

Published by Grove Press, Inc.
920 Broadway
New York, N.Y. 10010

Library of Congress Cataloging-in-Publication Data

Schneebaum, Tobias.
    Where the spirits dwell.

    1. Asmat (Indonesian people)   2. Schneebaum, Tobias.
3. Asmat (Indonesian people)—Sexual behavior.
4. Homosexuality, Male—Indonesia—Irian Jaya.
I. Title.
DU744.35.A82S37   1987   306.7'0899922   88-10715
ISBN 0-8021-0019-8

Designed by Irving Perkins Associates

Manufactured in the United States of America

First Edition 1988

10 9 8 7 6 5 4 3 2 1

to
Douglas Wright

ACKNOWLEDGMENTS

The author wishes to thank Claire Brook, Hayden Carruth, Berenice Cortelle, Allan Gurganus, Richard Selzer, Mona Simpson, Floriano Vecchi, William Weaver, and Douglas Wright for their readings of the manuscript, as well as my agent, Don Congdon, for putting up with my idiosyncrasies. The people of Asmat deserve special thanks, as do the Crosier Fathers and Brothers. Also to be thanked are the Corporation of Yaddo, the Ucross Foundation, The Virginia Center for the Creative Arts, and the Djerassi Foundation for giving me the time and place to work in peace and comfort, and to the Ingram Merrill Foundation for its generosity.

It is strange how mediocre all in civilization seems—art, journalism, philosophy, motion pictures, and even music, whenever I leave or "come out from" the New Guinea bush. I would have suspected the reverse—a sudden marvel at things cultural, at arts and letters, at civilized intercourse and accomplishments and yet time and again I have found them flat, disappointing, not up to expectations and woefully artificial. Perhaps it is their great remoteness from the real nature of man and his natural world environment that makes them appear flat and unreal.

Carleton Gajdusek
New Guinea Journal, 1961–1962,
Part Two

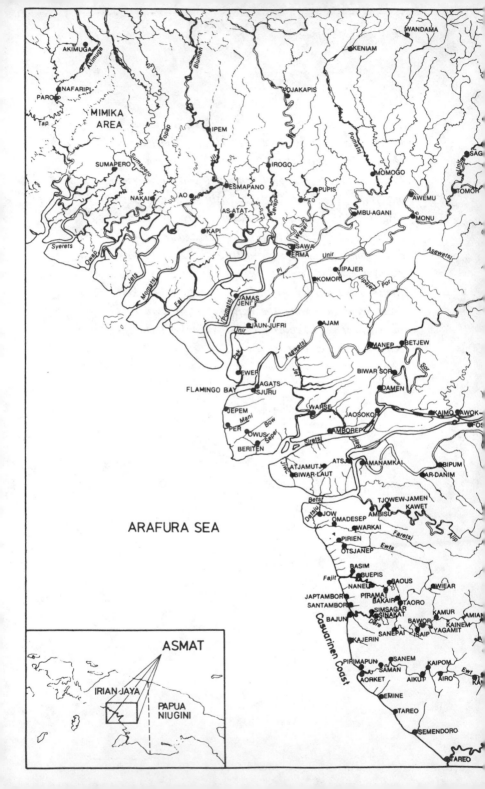

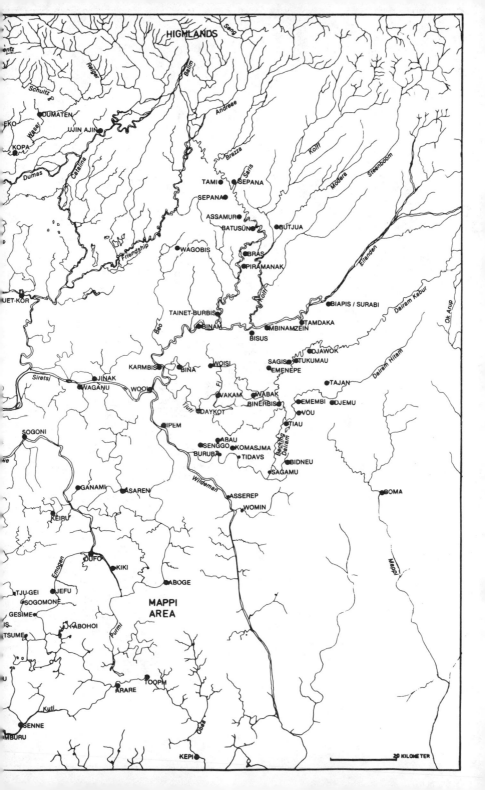

Chapter ONE

THEY had been so silent in their
approach that we had not heard their footsteps. They looked wild
and barbaric with their crocheted hair standing out in all directions, the black orbs of their eyes intense, fierce, full of bewilder-
ment and wonder. Some wore shell nosepieces. Most wore nothing
more than a pair of ragged shorts. All were timid, lacking the
courage to enter where the spirits dwell. They stared from the
entranceway at the great ancestor poles, one of which they immediately recognized as having been carved in their own village, with
figures named for their own recently dead relatives.

In New Guinea only a month, I stood in the doorway of the
museum with two friends, watching, listening.

"Uh! Uh!" they said, pointing up and down the pole, naming
sons, brothers, fathers, remembering the battle in which they had
been killed. Gathering heart at the presence of these familiar spirits, they moved into the room, went up to the pole that barely fit
into the twenty-foot space from floor to ceiling, and surrounded it.
Human figures and birds, painted red and white and black, had
been carved one above the other. From the groin of the uppermost
figure, a filigreed phallic wing projected. The whole of the pole
had been carved from a single mangrove tree, one of its ribbon
roots left intact, the tree turned upside down so that the flat root,
the penis, extruded from the top. It was a powerful affirmation of
virility and fertility, as if all the male spirits of the carving had
combined and were about to explode and ejaculate their life force
onto all below. Just as semen would burst from a phallus, so would
men burst from the men's house to raid an enemy village to avenge

the deaths of the ancestors depicted on the pole when it had first been carved.

"Kaper!" said one of the men, pointing to the carved figure that represented his younger brother.

"Satafin!" whispered another, his hand almost touching the figure below it, another relative killed in battle.

Men mouthed and whispered other names in awe almost inaudibly, identifying one by one all the ancestors on the pole. They pointed up to them or touched the lower ones tentatively, fearful the spirits might not yet have been satisfied in their quest for vengeance and still lived on in this alien room.

The men pressed themselves into a unit around the pole as if seeking the ancestors' protection against the spirits in the other artifacts on display, the shields and drums and spears. They whispered to one another, looked at us, leaned forward and said softly into our ears, "Otsjenep! Otsjenep!"—the name of the village they came from.

"Otsjenep!" said Trenk, advisor to the museum. "There you are, Tobias. That's where you wanted to go. Here is the perfect opportunity. Just go back with them."

"You're right!" I said. "Let's ask later."

The men unwrapped pandanus-leaf bundles and took out carved figures, bowls, and headrests and offered them for sale. We examined them carefully, complained of the poor quality of several but bought them all for the museum, hoping thereby to encourage the men to continue carving. The next time they came, I told them, we would be more selective and would reject work that had been hacked out too quickly, the carvings they had probably worked on the day before, when the decision had been made to go to Agats. When asked about my going to Otsjenep with them, Kas, the leader, nodded enthusiastically and said, *"Akato!"* Wonderful!

At daybreak the next morning, three painted and decorated men came to the mission and said they were ready to leave. At the edge of the walkway, four canoes were being loaded by crowds of men whose faces were streaked with red ocher and white lime. Many of them also wore headbands of cuscus fur, a marsupial the size of a large cat, with white feathers set in around them, and nosepieces of shell or human bone through their septa. All wore necklaces of dog teeth. They looked as if they were about to go on a raid.

Trenk—that is, Father Frank Trenkenschuh—immensely tall, thin, deeply tanned, wearing shorts and a T-shit that said "SHIT" in decorative capital letters, stood on the walkway above the channel into the Asewetsj River. "Hey!" he shouted. "You look like you're in the middle of a war party!"

Bram stood next to him, laughing. As curator of the museum, he was formally dressed in a long-sleeved batik shirt and long trousers. "Salamat jalan!" he said. "Have a good trip!"

Trenk yelled out, "Hey, Tobias! Your good friend Allo says goodbye. He doesn't expect to see you again. He's sure you'll be killed by these guys just like Michael Rockefeller! Salamat jalano! Bring me back some skulls!"

Kas, lean, with powerful shoulders and well-articulated chest and abdominal muscles, motioned me into his canoe. The goods that had been bought with money from the sale of the carvings— the shirts, shorts, dresses, fishing line, tobacco and flashlights— had already been loaded. The bows and arrows and spears had been placed on top of these, within easy reach. Kas had carefully arranged a place for me to sit, with my back against the patrol box in which I carried my canned goods and tobacco and other trade items. I sat there surrounded by the excitement of the men and filled with it, too. I waved at Trenk and Bram and yelled back "Salamat tinggal! Stay well!"

Without any sign or signal that I noticed, the men suddenly shouted in unison, "Uh!" They clacked their paddles against the sides of the canoes repeatedly, and then began paddling down the channel, one canoe behind the other. When we reached the Asewetsj, they lined up side by side, four canoeloads of men, all naked by then, each one having stepped out of his shorts as soon as we were away from the pier. They shouted, "Uh! Uh! Uh!" bending at the knees and working their paddles with such force that the canoe bounced up and down. They continued shouting to the rhythm set by the stroke of the paddles as we went from the mouth of the Asewetsj into Flamingo Bay. The Arafura Sea was ahead of us.

Had we gone straight on across the sea, had the men known what to expect and prepared themselves for the three-hundred mile journey, we would have reached the north coast of Australia. Instead, we turned east and kept as close to the shoreline as possible, avoiding waves that were higher than usual. It was early December, the month in which the northwest monsoon begins, a time rare for an Asmat to travel in the open sea. The men had been too thirsty for tobacco to wait through the full season of the monsoon before going to Agats to sell their carvings and had taken the chance. We were traveling along the southwest coast of what was formerly called Netherlands New Guinea, now known as Irian Jaya, a province of Indonesia, east of Borneo and Bali. The coast at this point is swamp for miles inland, the people are Asmat, Papuans like most people indigenous to New Guinea, black people with kinky hair, first seen by Westerners—the Portuguese explorers d'Abreu and Serrano—in 1511.

We had moved downstream quickly, swept along with the wind and the outgoing tide. The wind had been rising; its full strength struck as we moved out of the bay into the sea itself. The waves doubled in height but the men remained cheerful and even joked about the weather. A squall came up with chilling, heavy rain that knocked us about. I bailed with a sponge of shredded rattan and a scoop of sago spathe, that part of the sago palm leaf stem that grows from the trunk. Waves washed over us. We bounced on crests that sprayed cold as ice water. The men tensed their muscles against the storm and chanted, though their songs were lost in wind and rain.

The dugout was climbing high, lifted onto swells and then tossed down into hollows. In spite of the mist and rain screening out the world around us, I was suddenly aware that two of the men in our canoe were gone, thrown out by the violence of the sea. "Damn!" I thought. "Here it is again, another of those incidents like the Michael Rockefeller disappearance. Now the same thing is about to happen to us."

I laughed at the irony of the situation. I was, after all, traveling with the people of Otsjenep, the very people who were presumed by some to have killed Michael. If I disappeared, who would believe a story of drowning? No one in the canoe, however, seemed worried; in fact, everyone was laughing. Surprised at their good humor, I turned and looked back and saw the two missing men standing in swirling water barely reaching their waistlines, even though the shore was over two miles away. The Arafura Sea, off the coast of Asmat, was dangerously shallow for ships but was a blessing for paddlers thrown out of their canoes.

Kas, tired of paddling in such rough water, signaled for the canoes to turn landward. We were off the Boakap, a spit of land on which a bivouac had been built for those who wanted to spend the night while out fishing or on their way to Agats. It took an hour to reach the small shack that would shelter us, first paddling until there was no water to float us, then sliding the canoes over the mud. The tide was low and we sank to our knees as we pushed the canoes. The paddles were planted in the mire and the rattan ropes tied to them.

The rain had stopped for the moment. The men went into the forest for wood and fires were lit with matches I had given Kas. Everything was taken out of the canoes and brought into the bivouac. Pandanus mats were put down on the dry mud and we sat by the fires, warming ourselves. When we were settled, I gave Kas a plug of tobacco to distribute and everyone smoked. Balls of pounded sago, the pith of the sago palm, were put into the embers and turned with bamboo tongs. The outside was charred to a thick crust that was delicious when spread with the peanut butter and jelly I sometimes had with me, but otherwise dull and insipid. Inside the sago was a white mass that crumbled into small pieces, dry and tasteless. The men ate with obvious pleasure; it was, after all, their main food, their equivalent of bread and potatoes.

Rain thundered down again. The incoming tide that night brought water into the bivouac. Wind tore away the nipa palm leaves of the roof and rain poured down on us. We slept; we woke and moved our mats to drier spots; we woke, smoked, talked, tried to sleep again, but the rain and the rising tide swamped us. We sat closer to one another, smoking and talking, the wind howling around us. We became a tiny island of men huddled together for warmth, sheltering one another from the power of nature. Some of the men slept sporadically. Some talked and dozed. Before daybreak, the wind died down and the rain stopped. We slept again.

By midmorning, we were in the canoes traveling south with the curving coastline. The sun was covered with cloud and it was cold, but the skies soon cleared and brilliant sun warmed us. The men paddled slowly in the calmed sea. As the hours went by, the heat of the sun intensified and sweat covered their bodies. I opened a can of peaches, ate one, and gave the rest to the others.

The sun burned us, and even I, listless in the canoe, was feeling dehydrated. The men were quiet, paddling languidly, each one stopping now and then to smoke a cigarette lit with embers brought from the bivouac and passed along on paddle blade to paddle blade from one end of the canoe to the other. The air was opalescent, almost tangibly so. Perhaps it was the cold night with little sleep, the long day of paddling; perhaps it was the heat beating down on us, the slow swell of the sea, the shore birds sailing above us and plunging down for fish; perhaps it was the combination of it all that seemed to fuse into a nacreous atmosphere dimmed by our weariness. I almost reached out to touch the shell-like color of the air.

The coastline was close, feathery casuarina trees as well as mangrove growing there. Cuts in the forest were announced by Kas with the names of their small rivers. He turned to me from his place in front of the canoe and pointed ahead. *"Kali Sieh!"* he said. *"Kali Sieh!"* I could see a mound of mud billowing above the surface of the still water and, behind it, the narrow opening into the wall of trees that meant the Sieh River. Kas yelled to the men and they turned their dugouts toward the mud. The first canoe banked onto it and the men dove out. The other canoes slid up and everyone, suddenly enlivened, jumped out. A few minutes earlier, the men had been silent and sluggish, but there were no tentative movements; they dove headlong into the ooze, shouting as they leaped overboard. They screamed and howled, they yelped, whooped, laughed, swam, rolled around, jumped up and down, plopped in and out, filling the air with their shrill, raucous sounds. Boundless energy burst out as they expelled their passion. They were as if released from some great tension, as if there appeared a moment that had to be possessed and rejoiced in. They took it and gave into it, and wallowed in its delights. I too, watching the men, relishing their exuberance, dove out and wallowed in the cooling muck. I was sucked in, I sank and I plopped out. I screamed for the joy of it.

Kas threw globs of mud at me; I threw some back. He pushed me down for a moment and I couldn't breathe. He pulled me out and jumped on me. The sensuous slime, the hilarity of the men, their complete acceptance of the world around them and their openness, spontaneity, their giving into joy with all their senses was orgiastic. In the canoe, there had been calm and quietude; in the mud, there was a celebration of life. The change from those silent movements to the unrestrained display of pleasure instilled in me a new sense of my own limitations and I tried to expel the spirits that had restricted me. I gave myself fully to gratification.

The men, ready to leave, washed themselves in the water; I washed and smeared the mud from one place on my body to another. They dipped themselves into the sea and came up clean; I washed and the mud remained. Kas laughed and dumped me into the water, lifted me onto the rim of the canoe, threw water over me, rubbed at the mud, sprayed more water and rubbed again. I held onto his shoulders while he washed me. He laughed as the mud stuck to my pale, dry skin.

At dusk, in the distance at the edge of the sea, small black clouds of birds moved swiftly across the sky, crossing over each other, back and forth, as if not knowing in which direction to go. They seemed to flow through one another, then circle around and overlap. It wasn't until several evenings later that I saw them again on the Ewta River, thousands upon thousands of flying foxes, great swarms of them, flying down to the sea. Where were they going? What trees full of luscious fruit had they discovered?

It was night when we entered the mouth of the Faretsj River. Kas whispered, "We do not pass by Pirien. They fight with us. We go the upstream way." I had not realized that warfare continued between Otsjenep and Pirien, two halves of a single village in former times. They had fought over women and sago grounds and had separated. Both groups still lived on the Ewta River, Pirien downstream, Otsjenep upstream. We were going the long way around, taking an extra day.

We were traveling with the water, moving upriver with the incoming tide. No one spoke. Paddling had stopped, the paddles held upright in the canoes. We drifted soundlessly. The man at the stern steered. We came to the village of Omandesep, where we saw no fires, no torches, heard no sounds. Although we too were silent, the men were sharply alert, watching for any movement, any indication that attack might be imminent. It was in the darkness of night and early morning that raids on enemy villages took place.

War parties sometimes approached villages with friendliness, seeking sanctuary for the night; then, with everyone at ease and off-guard, they attacked, killed, or captured as many of their hosts as possible and took them into their canoes. It happened, too, that guests were welcomed lavishly with food and gifts and were later killed for the heads needed in initiation ceremonies or simply for revenge.

None of the men in the canoe smoked or spoke while we went by Omandesep. Past experience had taught them which villages they might go by without fear. We continued on for another hour, until we arrived at a small village. I learned the next morning, from the map that we had been in Warkai, an enclave of Sawi people who lived surrounded by the Asmat. In spite of differing customs, there was occasional intermarriage. Sawi men led us from the canoes into the small men's house where drumming and chanting had already begun. Inside, men and boys sat around five or six fireplaces and gossiped. I gave Kas tobacco which he broke into sections and handed to important men for further distribution. It was dark, difficult to see beyond the field of light thrown off by the fire at which we sat. Shields and drums, old ones, were brought out for me to look at, but I was too tired to see anything properly. I had already decided not to buy anything at night, when the light was poor. Later I regretted the decision, for we left at dawn.

Sago and shrimp were offered and we ate with pleasure. Kas, always aware of my ignorance of local customs, and always concerned with my well-being, put the shrimp into his mouth, cracked the shells, then peeled them before handing the flesh to me. The shrimp were huge and succulent, with no need for condiments. Satisfied, I unrolled my pandanus mat next to the fire to avoid the mosquitoes and immediately fell asleep. The men talked on.

"Tombias! Tombias!" Kas was whispering in my ear before long, waking me gently, fearful that my spirit, wandering outside my body at night, might not yet have returned. I was most vulnerable then, when anyone could easily kill me and my spirit would be damned, condemned to endless wandering, a dybbuk.

It was still dark when we loaded the canoes. The men of Warkai slept on while we tied our bundles, carefully avoided stepping over anyone and disturbing his spirit, and departed. The river was at the moment of changing tides, *air duduk* as the Indonesians say, "sitting water," just before it begins to rush down to the sea or begins to move upstream. On the blackness of the forest wall tiny lights burned, fireflies by the thousands on a single tree, not flickering on and off but burning steadily, an Asmat burning bush. I slept in the canoe, cramped, unable to stretch out my legs. It may have been the sunlight that awakened me; perhaps it was the soft chanting of the men:

> *Sisi ya*
> *yuwa sisi ya.*

The forest was so tight around us that the paddlers bent to avoid the outspreading branches. The water was already going down, the tide going out, when we turned south into the Wi River, where the forest unexpectedly changed into a swamp of huge grasses. The sky was open and expanding above our heads. Instead of woods, instead of pandanus and nipa palm and mangrove, there were immense grasses, pale green, different from the gloom and darkness of the forest. We were in a reed swamp that I hadn't expected, hadn't known about. Egrets and other wading birds were startled by our passage among them. In the channel through the reed, the grasses scraped and cut my arms, though the tough skin of the Asmat resisted injury.

It was not only the color, the varieties of green and the few blooming orchids that changed around us; sound, too, was different: the swishing of the leaves as we went by, the sharp clack of the paddles against cane stalks, the bird calls more like peeps than shrieks.

The men were regal, eloquent in movement, one standing behind the other, six, eight, or ten of them paddling easily on, singing;

> *Sisi ya*
> *yuwa sisi ya*
> *asa korama*
> *yi korama.*

A camaraderie existed, a covenant between the men in each canoe, ties of family mostly, brothers-in-law, bond friends, too. I watched them with yearning as they leaned into their paddles and chanted in unison:

> *Sisi ya*
> *yuwa sisi ya*
> *asa korama*
> *yi korama*
> *nana sisi wow*
> *nana sisi wow*
> *yi! yi!*
> *eh!*

> There are shrimp
> in the small river, there are shrimp
> they clean the shit

they clean the piss
we eat the shrimp
we eat the shrimp
yi! yi!
eh!

After that final, gutteral "eh!" the clacking of the paddles against the canoes began again. A sad, bemused expression was on the faces of the men, not violent at all but shyness there, soft and gentle, loving, it seemed, and tender-hearted. There was beauty that affected me deeply and I looked at the men and longed to put a hand to almost any cheek. There were harder faces, too, rough faces, grim with stubborn look, forbidding, austere, yet faces that could change and charm you in an instant.

We traveled on without time, without the need to arrive at daybreak or at dusk or at the exact hour of lunch. The tide was our timepiece; it alone regulated our schedule. Paddling was easiest with the current and all Asmat traveled with it, going upstream when the tide was coming in, downstream when it was going out. When we turned westward into the Ewta River, we were carried down by the stream flowing out to sea. It was then that the men blew their horns, when they felt safe again on their own river after the long journey through enemy territory to Agats and back.

"Hooo-ooo-ooo!" went the bamboo horns, three or four of them, each of a different pitch. "Hooo-ooo-ooo!" they declared, telling one and all of Otsjenep of the men's safe return. In another time, not long gone, the horns would have been announcing their return from a successful headhunting raid and the canoes would have carried dead bodies instead of goods from the shops of Agats.

During my years in Asmat, I often wondered what the men thought of when they paddled. At times, they appeared drowsy, paddling automatically, though even in that state I knew they were alert, aware of all that was going on around them, their eyes ever searching out opportunities for food and always wary of the possible approach of strangers. They scanned the forest continually for ripening fruit and watched for whatever disturbed the surface of life, no matter how small the splash of fish, how tiny the bird resting on a floating log, how faint the movement of an animal; they quickly identified all by shape and color, size and speed. Instinctively, they noted everything and stored away knowledge of streams, of birds, of their stands of sago, of dams and bivouacs, and of the traps for rats and marsupials. My own reaction time was more often than not too slow even to glimpse the crocodiles they pointed to before they slipped into the river. Did their minds at rest, I wondered, wander into the past to create and recreate events, seeing themselves as heroic warriors, great hunters of animals, fierce headhunters, too? Did they, like most of us, exaggerate their prowess and charms, looking back to see a past that fulfilled dreams instead of reality? Did any envision himself a great carver, a great lover? Did each man dream of vengeance on his enemies?

Later, while traveling on long journeys, I sometimes read, sometimes wrote in my journal, sometimes allowed my mind to drift into my past. I dreamed of the days to come and invented incidents I hoped would come to pass. I became one of the men in the canoe, strong and powerful, a familiar of the forest itself, of its trees, its birds, its animals. I knew how to make fire with a rattan loop and dried wood; I could build my house after a few machete slashes at a palm tree; I could protect my property and family with well-thrown spears and accurately directed arrows. I brought home wild boar once a month without ever receiving a scratch from the vicious tusks. I had even taken ten enemy heads and was respected by everyone, including my own four wives and twelve children. In my mind I was a universal man, capable of the greatest strength and endurance, just as I was capable of the greatest good.

In the canoe, I concentrated on the life of the forest, for it was always immediate, always to be seen and heard if you had Asmat eyes and ears or had the Asmat themselves to point it out. The silence of the canoe brought everything closer and the men were always relaxed.

On that first trip to Otsjenep, I began sorting out my life, as I had often tried to do without success. I watched the birds, the water, the trees, the sky, fixing in my mind the colors everywhere, the sea with its browns and reflected blues, the sky blue and red, purple, orange, changing every instant of daylight until that final flash of green at sunset, so startling it was difficult to believe. In that canoe on the way to Otsjenep, with the men fore and aft, myself in the center, it was as if the time had finally come to acknowledge myself as a human being, with my own power and place in the world. In the sereneness that came over me in the canoe, I could acknowledge that my goal was there around me at that moment and that while the men and the forest forced their presences onto me, I was at the same time watching myself in my youth studying Haftorah with our Hasidic rabbi, smelling the rancid odor of his black clothes that had pervaded the kitchen behind our grocery store in Brooklyn. I saw myself singing the blessings, sitting with him and singing them well even though I complained that my portion of the Torah was longest of all. I had taken easily to the notations of the chant and had no trouble. Although I never can sing Western songs and am always hitting wrong notes, I never had difficulty with Hebrew music. Rabbi never gave any indication of approval and often clumped me painfully on the head for any wrong vowel sound and when he did so, crumbs fell from his beard onto the pages of the book we read. I brushed them to the floor while he sat forward in his chair, hands on knees, his whole upper body nodding, rocking to the rhythm of his inner chant. I nodded in the canoe and sang to myself,

Baruch atah Adonai, Elohenu melech haolum.
Blessed be Thou, our Lord, King of the universe.

Was that music in the same key as *sisi ya*? Was that child sitting next to Rabbi the same me who now stood next to a naked black warrior, his nose stuffed with spiraling shell, his face painted white?

THE journey to New Guinea be-
gan on the subway, on the BMT, going from Manhattan to
Brooklyn after my father bought a grocery store on Third Avenue
and Sixty-eighth Street. I sat on the cane seats without fear, pro-
tected by my mother and my older brother, Moe. The apartment
from which we had just moved, far east on Thirteenth Street, is
vague to me now, for I confuse it with the roach-filled rooms in
which Sylvia Sydney lived in *Dead End*. But it is my source, the
wellspring; it is the point to which all roads from Europe led,
where my ancestors came together in the person of my parents who
brought me into a world from which I, never satisfied, have always
been escaping.

Of that first apartment, I remember only the kitchen floor covered with layers of patched linoleum, its checkerboard pattern of
green squares on white faded to nondescript colors. Silhouetted
against it is the bent figure of my mother mopping the floor, just
as she later mopped the linoleum on the floors of the three rooms
we had in the back of the store in Brooklyn.

We had been living on the Lower East Side next door to Aunt
Yetty, my mother's oldest and closest friend, and her husband Uncle
Adolph, and their daughter Ruth. It was Ruth who took care of us
because she was the oldest of us children. My younger brother
Bernie was not born until after we moved to Brooklyn. By then our
status had changed and my mother bore him in a hospital, though
she was back home the next day and the following day was again
working behind the counter. Years later, Ruth came to Brooklyn
and took us on a great expedition back to Manhattan to Radio City

Music Hall, where Shirley Temple was *Little Miss Marker* and the Rockettes were teapots with lids that became their hats.

My father arrived from Poland just before the First World War and took a job as a waiter in a Mt. Vernon resort hotel, the kind of place that flourished in the thirties, to which Orthodox Jews and Hasidim went to escape the summer heat of the city, if only for a few days. My mother arrived at about the same time, in 1913. Neither of them ever talked of their life in Poland or of their early days in *goldene* America, land of opportunity, or of New York with its streets paved with gold, a western land of milk and honey. They never talked of what it had been like traveling steerage amidst the smells of shit and rotting foods, vomit and urine, in the holds overstuffed with passengers. Only once did I physically experience anything that might have been comparable, aboard an Indonesian freighter going from Java to West New Guinea, three weeks on decks so crowded with immigrants that there was no way to lie down and stretch out, no way to avoid the stench from the two overflowing toilets meant to serve hundreds of men, women, and children. There was no water to drink, no water to wash with except what was brought up from the sea in buckets, and we were grateful for that. Whatever my attitude about those circumstances was then, I was not an immigrant escaping the oppression in Poland; I was not arriving penniless in an unknown land.

The earliest photograph of my father shows him in boot camp, in U.S. Army uniform during World War I. By enlisting, he had automatically become an American citizen. In the photograph he is stiff and awkward, with his hands hard against his thighs. His black hair is slicked straight back; his thick and sensuous lips are turned up in a smile that shows none of the violence of which he was capable. His calves are wrapped in khaki linen and he is thin, so different from the heavy man he later became. He hadn't married my mother yet, didn't until after the war, when he was selling eggs from a pushcart on Avenue B; my mother worked as janitor for several buildings on East Thirteenth Street, carrying the garbage and ash cans up from the cellars.

There are no photos of my mother from that time. She had long hair down her back that I later used to watch her brush, twist into a bun, and pin at the nape of her neck. It was a silky brown, verging on blond. She cut it off for Moe's *bar mitzvah,* kept it in a dresser drawer, then sold it when we needed money. She used a curling iron on her short, bobbed hair once a week, opening the prongs and rolling the hair between them.

She was a short woman and had the sweetest smile I've ever seen. She lit us up and comforted us with that smile. She never complained to us of anything, not even of my father's constant verbal attacks, when he insisted that she could never do anything right. But I loved her and she could do no wrong. There were never any peaceful moments when my father was at home, except when he sat at the kitchen table weeping over a story in the *Jewish Daily Forward.* I used to watch his tears and wonder why he expended such compassion on characters in stories but not toward his wife and children. There was never any indication of love or affection between my father and mother, nor any indication that he might love his children.

My father's friends loved him. With them he could be generous and easy. He played cards with them and lent money that was never returned. He went to the market several times a week and made extra money candling eggs. Moe and I both learned to candle in the back of the store, in the tiny dark room near the kitchen. I felt very proud when I was able to roll three eggs in one hand in front of the light bulb. Every other Sunday night, my father's gang came to play pinochle. It was a big event for me and my brothers and we were allowed to watch the play and the coins being tossed into the pot. They played at our round oilcloth-covered table, the one on which we ate and at which we did our homework, and studied Hebrew after school with our bearded rabbi.

The earliest photos of my mother were taken at a photographer's studio and show the five of us, and my Uncle Harry, who had come from Europe to live with us. Uncle Harry married his first cousin Ann Waldman, whom the family disliked because she smoked cigarettes, wore makeup, and flirted with men. Uncle Harry and Ann (she was never dignified with the title "aunt") lived with us in our three rooms and had a baby that died two weeks after its birth. Ann screamed for twenty-four hours and tried to tear her hair out by its roots. She and Uncle Harry moved out when my father bought another store and Uncle Harry ran it for him. They never had any more children. When Uncle Harry died, Ann screamed again, and again tried to tear clumps of hair from her head. She jumped into Uncle Harry's grave and screamed and pounded on the coffin until she was carried away, her arms flailing and her legs kicking the air. She remarried a year later and that husband died after a few months. She remarried twice again and buried those husbands, too. I lost interest in her after Uncle Harry's death when I watched my older brother put his hand inside her halter and caress her breast.

My father bought a third store and put his first cousin Phil Ringle in charge. Ringle, as my father called him, sold the goods and kept the money for himself, claiming business was bad. He had been constantly rearranging the canned goods on the shelves so it was impossible to see that there was nothing behind the stock in front. He ran away to Bridgeport, deserting his wife and two children. With the stolen money, he opened a fur store that was so successful he opened a factory that produced mink and sable coats. None of us ever saw him again and he never returned my father's money. The news eventually reached us that he had a weekly radio program on the Polish station and regularly made anti-Semitic speeches.

I never knew where Phil Ringle, Aunt Yetty, my parents, or any of the family came from, except that it was eastern Poland, somewhat near Przemysl. If I'd ever known the name of the villages I cannot now dredge them up.

Uncle Bernie arrived in the mid-1930s on the S.S. *Pilsudski*, which docked in mid-Manhattan. He came as a stowaway, hidden in a closet from the day the ship left Gdynia. He walked down the gangway in a steward's jacket into my mother's arms. He had no baggage. He was about twenty-two and had the same appealing look on his face that my mother had; I loved him the moment he appeared. He and Uncle Harry were my mother's brothers. He too lived in the back of the store with us until he married. He got a job immediately pressing rubber molds, and had great blisters on his hands that took months to turn into calluses. He received the low salary usually paid to illegal aliens. Even so, he took me to my first opera, *Faust,* with Helen Jepson, and introduced me to the singing of Jarmila Novotna and Jan Kiepura. He took me to the movies and we went out riding in his old Ford until he began taking out girls on Saturday nights. He had a bumpy nose, just like Uncle Harry, a variation of my mother's hooked one. He married Belle, of whom the family also disapproved because she used words like shit all the time. They moved to another part of Brooklyn, had two children, finally moved to a retirement village in Ft. Lauderdale.

My father's official name in English was Jacob but everyone called him Yankle. My mother never had an English equivalent for Riftcha, a corruption of Rivka, the sound of which confused the registrar at school. Sometimes, we wrote down Rebecca, sometimes Rose; we were never consistent with her name. I went through all my school years as an impostor, using the name Theodore, a.k.a. Ted. When my mother took me to P.S. 102 and said my name was Toivele, eyebrows were raised and Theodore was written down in its place. I had no idea I was legally Tobias until I needed a passport and had to produce identification papers. Most of my family still call me Ted, even though I have been Tobias for over forty years.

The neighborhood in which we lived in Brooklyn was Scandinavian. It changed only slightly during our first years there. The Izzo family moved in next door and opened a hardware store. The old people didn't speak English and never learned any. They planted rose bushes in their back yard and made a proper garden. Our back yard was less cultivated. Uncle Bernie was interested in gymnastics and got us to sink two tree trunks into the ground and put up an iron crosspiece so that we had a horizontal bar. He taught me tricks and I learned to hang from my heels, to swing around from my knees and finally swing full circle with my arms extended. The Schwartzes moved in on the other side of the Izzos and had a tailor shop and three daughters. Sylvia, the middle daughter, invited me to her high school prom but it was Moe who later married her. Dottie, the youngest daughter, taught me tap dancing as she was learning it and we did the "shuffle off to Buffalo" and other dances down the street.

My mother died of uterine cancer when she was about thirty-eight. Uncle Harry, younger still, died of cancer ten months later. Moe had his first bowel cancer operation before he was forty. Ten years later he had a colostomy and died a few years after that. Bernie had two operations for the same thing and recently had a second malignant brain tumor removed. I've been lucky enough to get away with only one operation so far. Jeffrey, Bernie's middle child, was having pains in his stomach when he was fourteen or fifteen. He went through the usual tests for cancer and after his barium enema said, in his casual way, "Well, now I really feel I'm a member of this family." Fortunately, there was nothing seriously wrong with him.

Moe was the smartest and most studious of the three of us. He was a genius in mathematics, his major at City College, upsetting my father who had expected him to become a wrestler. Moe was heavier than the rest of us, a fact that made him seem suitable for the sport in my father's eyes. My father went to the matches twice a week at Ft. Hamilton, Tuesdays for wrestling, Thursdays for the fights. Moe got one of the highest marks ever recorded on the I.Q. test when he went into the army. We couldn't help but laugh when he was made an M.P. and guarded German prisoners-of-war in the States. He applied for officer's training but was turned down because of poor eyesight; he wore thick, steel-rimmed glasses. Eventually he was transferred to the Signal Corps as a lineman, always preceding the troops in conflicts like the Battle of the Bulge. After the war he worked for the government and ended up at NASA, which sent him back to school for a Ph.D. at M.I.T. He designed and built the first American satellites, the SAMOS and the TYROS. His ERS, the Earth Resources Satellite, was sent up shortly after his death and is still circling the earth and sending back information on minerals below the surface. He had always fascinated us with stories of what he was working on, but I was particularly astonished the day he said simply, "I fired G.E. yesterday. They've been making too many mistakes." NASA established the Moe Isaac Schneebaum Award in 1975, given every year to an outstanding young physicist. If ever I thought of myself as an explorer of the unknown, I had only to remind myself of Moe's mind encompassing the universe to put my naïve conceits into proper perspective.

Neither Bernie nor I could compete in any sense with Moe and we were smart enough to recognize it, though there was nothing about Moe that would provoke a sense of competition. Bernie had a relatively good life for himself and for his wife and three children, beginning as a salesman. After his first brain operation, he was forced into retirement. In the army, he had been stationed in such remote places as India and Bahrain Island. I had been a radar mechanic, mostly at Baer Field in Ft. Wayne, Indiana, but I was also in camps in California, Arkansas, Missouri, Texas, and North Carolina, never in any danger.

After the war, I worked in my father's grocery store on Eighty-sixth Street in Brooklyn and went to the Brooklyn Museum Art School at night to study with Rufino Tamayo. He was a fine man but a poor teacher. He had all of the students turning out bad Tamayos. It was he who convinced me to go to Mexico in 1947, rather than to Paris. "Nothing there now," he said. "Mexico is much more interesting." I went to Mexico and stayed almost four years and got my first taste of primitive life, visiting the Lacandon Indians, a group discovered by Frans Blum in 1947. They were living traditional lives in the forest of Chiapas, close by the ruins of Bonampak. I went on horseback to a hamlet of three houses and found fifteen men, women, and children, all with long unkempt hair and wearing dirty, shiftlike, homemade garments. I was with them for only a couple of weeks but there was something basic in their way of life that attracted me, even though they were physically unappealing in my eyes and had no impulse toward cleanliness.

Later, I lived for a time in Peru with men who, at first, represented to me the "noble savage." I had been drawn in by the closeness of the men to one another, living and loving in small groups within a huge house, in which all the villagers dwelt. The women and children inhabited the central section, while the men slept close to the walls, surrounding them in the oval-shaped building. I lived with a group of six men, spending nights in the close-knit bundle of them, an integral part of their interweaving arms and legs. My naïveté and unawareness glossed over the areas of their lives that I did not or would not understand. The people were not controlled by our Judeo-Christian ethic but by their own customs. It was only after being with them for several months that I saw that they were as limited and controlled as we in the Western world and that they, too, had violence in their lives that troubled me. I had blocked out everything that negated my concept of the noble savage and when that became too well-defined to be ignored, I left.

Peru was a powerful experience. In order to begin to understand the demons in me, I thought to write a book that might absorb those furies and thereby leave me free. In telling the tale of a time when I was almost always with men (the women lived peripherally, as far as my contact with them was concerned), I learned how desperate I had always been for precisely the kind of relationship I found for myself there—a physical closeness to men, even convergence, yet with distance between us in mind and emotion, a noninvolvement in the most basic experience of shared love and passion, suffering, pain, and affliction. The men themselves were surely capable of all but the first of those attributes, and perhaps that one too. I never understood it in myself. My relationship with those men was no more than an extension of the temper of my time with X, a relative I loved in childhood who had permitted certain liberties on my part, had even encouraged them, but never reciprocated. The very moment I needed acknowledgment most he remained silent and elusive, never allowing himself to bridge with his eye the short gap between us.

Am I, then, the result of those limited encounters? Did I see myself as never being close to anyone? Was I, with those men, taking on the role that X had imposed on me, of sympathy and affection, but never permitting love? Had love, in fact, ever come my way? Was I, am I, capable of extending myself in that way? Is it only now that my body has settled and been relieved of the burden of what I thought of as my continuing search for the unknown that love has become possible? Is it now love or is it simply age looking back at an emptiness I had sought to fill by escaping the present, by going on, pretentiously hoping to go deeper into untouched areas of myself? I do now move into untapped regions, where I had never thought to go. Love has girded my loins, urged me on into new visions.

The book I wrote on Peru had its exaggerations. It had never occurred to me as I was writing that anyone would be interested in what I had to say. I wrote it as I felt it, changing time elements and adding to the number of those my friends had killed in their quest for vengeance. Yet I wrote truly, truthfully, about the life I lived. I look back now at the simplicity and naïveté of myself and wonder who I was and where I had come from.

I went on from Peru, of course. I lived, worked, moved, made friends, and changed. I went to Peru on a Fulbright and when I returned to New York had burst out onto canvas and shown my paintings at the Peridot Gallery. I went to Greece and Italy, crossed Asia by land, went to Africa. Each time I returned when I ran out of money, worked at folding Christmas cards for Tiber Press, painted and exhibited. I had friends and sometimes I thought I was in love; yet there was never enough love on my part to keep me in one place.

Chapter

THREE

AGATS, capital of Asmat, had a population of a little more than four hundred when I first arrived the summer of 1973. The people were mostly outsiders— Indonesians from other islands who were government officials, traders and merchants, plus a few Asmat in the army and police, together with groups from other parts of what was then called West Irian. It was an intensely romantic-looking place, with wooden houses on poles above the water and mud, and raised walkways lined with coconut trees. At daybreak the light was cold and gray, often still full of the heavy rain that normally fell at night and eased off at dawn, when the dark sky would be suddenly pierced by streaks of sunlight, with patches of blue appearing as the clouds dissolved. The sun lit up the trees first, then the corrugated tin roofs, blinding the flying foxes that had squeaked during the night as they flew from palm to palm gorging themselves on coconuts. The light was harsh during the day and the walkways empty until late afternoon, when I and others strolled and gossiped and looked into houses and inside the three shops (which ten years later increased to twenty and more, just as the population quadrupled). I sat at the pier each evening, sometimes alone, sometimes with a friend, watching the golden sky ripple with changing color, yellows turning into reds and purples, and finally resting for a few hours in Prussian blue prickled with stars, until the rains came and cast somber browns and blacks like veils over the night.

The Indonesian residents wore their tight skin in richly varied chromatic colors, from the darkest browns of the Asmat and their fellow Papuans to the ochers and russets, madders, and magentas of the Javanese, the Makasarese and the people of Bali and

23

Sumatra. How different and insipid the pale pink and blanched sienna of the Western missionaries!

The town of Agats itself is on the left bank of the Asewetsj River, just above where it opens out into Flamingo Bay, so named for the first ship to enter its waters, the M. V. *Flamingo*. The land, like almost all of Asmat, is low and flat with tidal waters rising to cover most of it, sometimes once a day, sometimes twice, a curiosity of single and double tides each month, rare on earth. At low tide, the sea is shallow for miles out from the indistinct shoreline, and the great stretches of mud seem like vast barren basins, moors of soilless mire over which men and women easily slide their canoes on their way to and from their fishing grounds and stands of sago. The huge rivers that run through Asmat have their source in the mountains and streams issuing forth everywhere, although it is a land of peat bog and mud, not true land at all but a swamp of mangrove trees and sago palms, of ironwood and soft-wood trees, with delicate casuarina at the edge of the sea farther south.

Also in Agats were the Crosiers, members of the Order of the Sacred Cross, founded in Belgium at Clairlieu, outside Huy, in 1210. I had been prepared to dislike them one and all, though I hoped to use them for my own purposes in traveling around. I was prejudiced: missionaries had always seemed arrogant and destructive to me, wanting to impose their own conceits onto others as if there were no other ways of life, or other ways to what they thought of as God and religion. Fourteen of them lived in Asmat at that time, the greater part scattered through the coastal regions. They had come from the Midwest, from South Dakota and Minnesota and Colorado, and points farther east like Michigan, Indiana, and Pennsylvania. Two had been in Asmat for more than fifteen years.

The Catholic mission was presided over by Bishop Alphonse August Sowada, a cheerful, intelligent man with an understanding and sympathy for the local people as well as for his Crosiers, though not all would agree with my judgment. I knew nothing then, of course, about the Asmat or its people, and nothing about the outsiders who lived there.

It was through the bishop, however, and Father Frank Trenkenschuh that I happened to stay and work in Asmat. I had gone there as a traveler after a month among the Dani in the highlands of Irian Jaya, where I found myself frequently bored. The Dani were stimulating at first, but there was something unsatisfactory in my relationship with them. Perhaps I was not capable then of close contact with anyone. I wanted to experience something immediate and intense with the men in the men's house, even within the short time of my stay. I did not think what I might offer them, only what they might offer me. The men wore long gourd penis sheaths that were tied down at the testicles and were held erect by a string around the waist; they wore pig tusks through their noses and breast decorations of nassa shells tied tightly at the neck like dickeys. Their matted hair and shining bodies dripped with pig grease, and many had red or black paint on their faces and white feathers in their hair. They were short in stature, brawny, with thickly muscled thighs and calves. They were always congenial and helpful but I was an outsider and felt like one, always apart, always outside life, not even a good observer. The women were far removed in every sense, sleeping separately and working separately in the fields of sweet potatoes. Their skirts were tied so low on their hips that their buttocks were bare. The long string bags in which they carried babies, food, and firewood, stretched from their foreheads down their backs and covered the rump.

Maybe my feeling was nothing more than a memory of tantalizing places pushing me on to Asmat, a memory of photographs I'd seen of Asmat men, naked and wild, of carvings rough and crudely made, powerful and magnetic, the people and art exuding an energy that attracted and agitated me. Perhaps it was nothing more than the thought that what lay on the other side of the mountain was more exciting than what was immediately around me.

Photographs often lie and exaggerate; they can be taken from odd angles and odd viewpoints; they can be seen with jaundiced eyes or from prejudiced conceptions. I had looked at photographs of Asmat and had seen what I wanted to see; cannibals and head-hunters who might absorb me into their lives.

I had lived before with people who had little or no contact with the outside world—the Lacandon in Chiapas, a group of Mashco in the Madre de Dios of Peru, the Murut of North Borneo, and the Ifugao of Luzon—people who had stimulated me in ways that profoundly affected my sensibilities. They had brought out emotions and powers that had been latent and needed only the spark of what I thought of as freedom to ignite and unleash forces that would allow me complete self-expression and therefore happiness.

I was always searching for freedom and fulfillment without ever knowing what the words meant. On the printed page and in my mind, they meant Rousseau and Diogenes, Archimedes, Socrates and St. Augustine, Bernanos and Mahatma Gandhi, a mixture of truth and love, never definable, found only in some distant, uncorrupted people far from the influence of Western ways. I was painting and exhibiting then in New York; I was reading *The Tale of Genji,* the *Zohar,* Agatha Christie, the *Mahabharata,* James Hanley, *The Dream of the Red Chamber,* Isaac Babel, and Martin Buber. I was going to the Metropolitan Opera House, standing at the top, listening to great music and great voices. Still, I felt vacant, not yet furnished.

Friends in New York accepted and loved me, but what they gave me—what I allowed myself to take from them—was never enough to stop whatever forces drove me on to foreign lands. Whatever that urgency was that made me move, it could not have sprung whole from me like Athena from the head of Zeus. If I think back to my childhood, I see now that the first of my journeys was nothing more than a continuation of other journeys, that I come from a long line of travelers, that through my genes I am a descendant of that tribe who have been wandering since God threw them out of the Garden of Eden.

The bishop, one of those with whom I became most friendly in Asmat in the years that followed, was born in a farm community near St. Cloud, Minnesota, of Polish/German ancestry, one of eight children, the most restless of them, the one who never sat still or stayed in one place.

"He was forever running off to visit his friends on neighboring farms instead of doing his daily chores," his mother said to me one day. I had gone to St. Cloud to take part in the celebration of the bishop's twenty-fifth anniversary in the priesthood in 1983. "He would never stay home and do his work. He was maddening, believe me. Once, because he had gone gallivanting much earlier than usual, I was so angry when he came home that I stuffed his head in a bucketful of water for longer than I care to remember." Yet, in spite of conflicts, theirs was a loving family.

One of the missionaries once said to me, "You know, the bishop was always known as Dirty Al, first because he was so comparatively short that when he played games like basketball, he fouled with his hands all the time; then, he was Dirty Al because of his foul language."

Alphonse Sowada was elevated to his high position as bishop of the diocese of Agats/Asmat in 1969, after eight years as pastor of the village of Sawa and later as superior in Agats. He was thirty-six at the time, the youngest man in the Catholic church ever to be so ordained.

On my first visit to his house in Agats, his warmth and friendliness put me at ease immediately. He welcomed me with a comforting smile on his unlined face, a resolute but cordial handshake, and a cold can of Tiger beer. He was not at all the pious, self-satisfied religious I was used to meeting. He thoroughly enjoyed where he was and what he was doing, and he enjoyed the people themselves, their way of life and the things they produced. His grin and flashing blue eyes reminded me of those cherubim in the paintings of Annibale Carracci, all innocence at first glance, but always with a sparkle of humor and a hint of mischievousness.

He was generous with his time and offers of help. And, when I mentioned the fact that I was a painter and was interested in artifacts, insisted that I be taken into the museum the mission was building. It was Father Trenkenschuh who took me there, thereby changing my life.

* * *

If the men of Otsjenep had been awed, terrified, and excited by what they saw in the museum and by the spirits they knew were there, my own first experience with the carvings inside the museum was equally remarkable. It was as if I'd walked into an invisible wall that had knocked the breath out of me. I could not feel what the Asmat felt in the presence of objects in which their ancestors were embodied, but I was struck by the presence of works that powerfully expressed their owners' feelings and, in wood, paint, feathers, and seeds, represented their experiences in a world inhabited by ancestral spirits that were ever-present until forced on to the land of the dead. The carvings asserted themselves and demanded attention.

There was no way for me then to take in what I was looking at—the ancestor poles, shields, drums, figure carvings, body masks, and bamboo horns. I could only stand there, hoping to absorb bit by bit something of what they were and meant. I went to the museum again the next day and every day I was in Agats, ingenuous, inexperienced, knowing nothing of the meaning of the carvings, only the power they held over me. I was caught in their magic, as if they had cast a spell that charmed me. I knew I was susceptible to sorcery and saw it clearly in myself months later during a feast in the village of Ajam, Trenk's village, as I stood on the bank of the Asewetsj at four in the morning. The heavens were without light, though somewhere in the distance dawn was easing itself through clouds of black and purple, a sliver in the tenebrous sky. On the far side of the river, movement on the water's still surface drew my attention, and I saw the ghost of a canoe with two paddlers, one at each end, and in the center a spirit enshrouded in a mask of woven rattan and shredded leaf. The form was indistinct in that light, at that distance; it stood in the center of the canoe, head bowed, unmoving, enveloped in an aura that blocked out the paddlers and the canoe itself. It was as if floating on the water, an ancestral spirit moving silently, inevitably toward the bank, the river's surface showing no ripples, the light coming up behind the spirit, creating a halo around it, the mood of its stance electrifying. I was caught up in its presence, accepting the waves it sent out to terrify us all. I felt myself inside the Asmat world, believing implicitly in the spirit's destructive force and its ability to cleanse the village of all evil. It did not matter that the canoe landed and I could see the feet of the man who wore the mask; I accepted its truth and spirituality, and it wasn't until hours later that its effect on me wore off.

I traveled as much as I could during the three months of my first stay in Asmat, seeing something of what the people were like and arriving in one village in time for a scarification ceremony during which the arms of young girls between the ages of seven and twelve were being burned. A stick was taken from the fire, its end glowing, was pressed into the girls' flesh from wrist to shoulder, producing double rows of wounds that later festered and turned into circular keloids. In another village I was adopted by a man, his two wives, and an unknown number of their children. The ritual required that I suck the nipples of my new father and mothers, one of whom had a great part of her face eaten away by yaws. I wondered only for an instant about the lesions being contagious before bending to suckle at the dry breasts. It was only after the ceremony that I learned that being adopted meant giving gifts to my family.

In the museum itself I talked to the curator, Bram Kuruwaip, a Muyu from the foothills of southeastern Irian Jaya, and quickly learned how differently people saw themselves even in New Guinea. "The Muyu have big asses," Bram said. "Just look at mine. It is beautiful, not at all like those of the Asmat. Among us, the worst insult is to call someone 'small ass'! Here in Asmat it works the other way around. Don't call anyone 'big ass' or you'll end up in a big fight." Eric Sarkol, Bram's assistant, born in Merauke of parents who came from the Kei Islands, had other ideas on the subject and believed himself superior to all Asmat because the Keiese have a lighter skin color, are "real" Catholics, and can read and write.

I talked most of all to Trenk when he invited me to spend a few days at his house in Ajam, a village an hour and a half by outboard up the Asewetsj. Through him I began to feel accepted, at least by the Westerners. Two hundred feet from the river, the house was supplied by generator with electricity at night, though Trenk often did not turn it on, and had comfortable couches and chairs and two tiny guest rooms. On the walls and doors were mottos new to me: WARNING! said one of them, over the doorway to his own bedroom, I AM NAKED UNDERNEATH MY CLOTHES! A sign above the doorway of one of the other bedrooms said HONK IF YOU'RE HORNY! On the way to the back porch was STREAKERS TAN MORE EVENLY, as well as the complementary NOT ALL STREAKERS ARE CREATED EQUAL. Two more in the bathroom, both written with a felt-tip pen, kept the visitor thinking while shaving (women guests were put up in one of the married teacher's houses): ONLY A FOOL WOULD LOOK INTO A MIRROR AND EXPECT A WISE MAN TO RETURN HIS STARE and IF YOU DON'T EXPECT THE UNEXPECTED, YOU'LL NEVER FIND IT. A few seconds' look around the house was enough to make it obvious that Trenk was no ordinary priest, no ordinary missionary.

I first saw him on the walkway in Agats, surrounded by a crowd of youngsters, students at the junior high school, several of them hanging onto his arms or hugging his thighs, all adoring him. He was telling them about a magical device he would bring back the following year. "You wait and you'll see the machine. You wait until next year. You'll see men and women and children walking around as if they were in the same room with you. They'll even be talking. And you'll see houses so big, everyone in Ajam could live in a single one of them. They could all eat and sleep there. You wait and you'll even see animals so big you could ride them." None of the kids seemed to believe this outrageous story and they all laughed and punched at Trenk, but they also knew him well enough to know that something extraordinary would be coming.

Later that day Trenk and I sat in the mission recreation room, drinking beer. Almost without preliminary, he said, "It's not that corruption is a way of life in Indonesia, it is *the* way of life, and it is my job to teach the Asmat to cope with this." It was a statement that shocked me, that seemed too defeatist an attitude, yet was one that endeared him to me for life. All he said that day was confirmed later when I saw the relationship between the Indonesians and the Asmat.

Trenk was slender in 1973, without the huge stomach he gradually developed. He was, however, a huge man by any standards, imposing partly because of his six feet four inches and partly because of his splendid good looks. He was only in his mid-thirties then, but his hair was already turning white, giving him a distinguished air. His jaw was square, his eyes blue, brilliant, searching, his smile sweet, and he had the kind of broad humor that was close to that of the bishop. He talked a lot about his childhood, most often about how he and his sister had constantly harassed their "mom" and played practical jokes she didn't appreciate because they so often destroyed household objects and broke bones.

In spite of his outward appearance of strength, good will and geniality, there was a surprisingly dark and vulnerable side to Trenk. He seemed bold and independent but, in truth, he was badly in need of reassurance and hope. He was defenseless at times and easily offended when others disagreed with what was called "his pronunciamentos" and his recommendations. He also had a fiery temper. Nearly everyone there, including Trenk himself, took pleasure in telling me a long, involved story about that temper, an episode that took place before I arrived in Asmat. I never understood the whole of it, mostly because everyone told a different version.

Trenk admits to having gone into a fury one Sunday when he learned that the people of Ajam were in almost continuous wife exchange for ritual purposes. In his anger, he picked up the church's cross and threw it into a muddy ditch. He told the people that their behavior was like throwing Christ Himself into the ditch, just as he had done with the cross. His parishioners were horrified, unable to imagine a religious object being treated in this way. They took up the cross, cleaned it, and tried to return it. Trenk would not accept it, he said, until they assured him that all wives were permanently back with their true husbands. Indignant discussions and wrathful words flew back and forth for days. Finally, the people, somewhat hesitantly, told Trenk that wife exchange had stopped.

Even with disagreements between Trenk and his people, he remains the only missionary in Asmat known to all and called to his face by his Asmat name, Wasanipitsj, Jungle Man, a name given to him because he regularly accompanied his villagers into the forest when they went in search of food or a hiding place from government troops looking to press them into service cutting wood.

Years later, Trenk, on one of his visits home to the U.S., went into therapy for six months. He returned to Asmat with a renewed sense of his worth, a renewed sense of hope, and of the mission itself.

Such were my introductions to Asmat. Everything intrigued me. In fact, I was so overcome by the carvings and the people that I decided to find a way to return. I asked Trenk who would be cataloguing the artifacts in the museum. No one, he said. There was no one capable of doing it. Trenk, as advisor to the museum, and the bishop, as director, agreed that I might return as a volunteer when I offered to train myself in the United States. I left for New York shortly thereafter and registered for courses leading to a degree in cultural anthropology. I was lucky in making contact with Douglas Newton, then Director of the Museum of Primitive Art* (where I was also able to study card cataloguing systems), and with Dr. Rhoda Metraux, Research Associate of the American Museum of Natural History, both of whom consented to be my teachers.

After my first year of studies, I went back to Agats in 1975 to work on the catalogue and on my thesis, eventually receiving my degree in 1977. Just before I left New York, Dr. Metraux suggested that I take along the Lowenfeld Mosaic Test. "It is a test that anyone can do," she said, "aimed at understanding groups of people throughout the world. It shows how people go about a task and the styles of men, women, and children of all generations. It is

* Now, Chairman of the Department of Primitive Art at the Metropolitan Museum of Art.

used in psychological and cultural analyses, and in cross-cultural comparisons." In this test a series of 228 plastic tiles in six different colors: white, green, black, yellow, blue, and red, and five different shapes: squares, equilateral triangles, diamonds, isosceles triangles, and scalene triangles, are arranged on a board in whatever manner the subject desires. No hints are given concerning the possibilities of arrangement of the tiles, which could be placed one next to another rather than fitted together as in a jigsaw. I decided to practice on the crew of the Indonesian freighter on which I sailed from New York to Jakarta. My first subject was the assistant cook. I laid out the tiles according to shape and color and told him to put as many or as few as he liked onto the board in any way that pleased him. He was slow picking up the tiles, trying each one in different places before making a final decision. About three-quarters of an hour later, he had made a house with two windows and a door. I thanked him and sent him on his way, admonishing him not to reveal anything whatsoever about the test to any of the crew or officers. Alone in my cabin, I put a piece of transparent paper over the design and carefully traced all the tiles and wrote onto each one the chosen color. It took two hours to complete that first test. Later I was able to manage more quickly. Over the next several days, the captain, one of the mates, and a group of seamen came into my cabin one by one. Each produced something easily recognized by me—birds, animals, flowers, human figures.

In Asmat, my first testing was on the eighteen-year-old who worked for the bishop. Bram, the curator of the museum, gave the directions we had worked out in Asmat. The young man picked up one tile, then another and another, rejected one, picked up another. He picked up several more and held them all in one hand, then put them in the center of the board in a stack of eleven that included all colors. He took another group of the same height and stacked them next to the first pile. Later that day we tried it with two more Asmat, who also stacked them up. Several times during my first year, I tried the test with Asmat men, women, and children of all ages. No one put them flat, next to one another, in the expected two-dimensional manner.

This inability to understand two-dimensional shapes or characters brought to mind an article by Anthony Forge, about the art of the Abelam, the people with whom he lived in Papua New Guinea. The forms they paint on flat surfaces, he wrote, may look like human figures to us, but were not meant to do so; instead, they were designed to represent various manifestations of humans. Although they painted these symbols in two dimensions, they had no understanding of photographs after more than twenty years of contact with Westerners. "Their vision," Forge explained, "has been socialized in a way that makes photographs especially incomprehensible, just as ours is socialized to see photographs and indeed to regard them as in some sense more truthful than what the eye sees." Thus, for the Asmat, the medium of the mosaic test was completely unsuited to their visual and thinking processes.

Chapter

FOUR

SO it was 1975 when Trenk set me on the path I was looking for. I would be taking many such trips in the future, for I was in Agats a total of four years, from 1973 when I first arrived until mid-1983 when I completed the research and card catalogue that I had volunteered to do for the museum. That first collecting trip to Otsjenep, however, was unique: it was the beginning of a time of learning that taught me not only about the Asmat but myself as well.

Kas and I and the others were then on our third day of travel, approaching Otsjenep. The mist had cleared early and the day was brilliant with sun. I peered ahead through tall reeds looking for signs of human life but there was nothing obvious, nothing to indicate to me that people lived within miles. We stopped abruptly at a bank sloping up from the river. Kas motioned and called "*Ndei! Ndei!* Come!" We walked along a narrow path, filled with mottled gray logs, rotting twigs and foliage skirting deep mud. In front of us were trees rising behind translucent spear grass. High up were two houses atop thin poles, both reached by ladders of sticks tied together with rattan. The lower house was about twenty feet above the ground.

Youngsters of all ages, most of them wearing nothing, came to carry our goods. There were no greetings, no hellos, no signs of welcome; nor were there any from the women who were looking down from the doorways; Asmat women show no affection for their husbands in public. Between the ladders was a small pool of water in which Kas swirled his feet before going up to the higher house. I followed. The rungs were unevenly spaced and so far apart it was

35

difficult to climb, though later I watched young children and women with babies and firewood on their backs mount with ease.

Kas showed me where to sit and where to put my gear, in what I took to be his own living area. It was dark and empty inside. The women who had been looking down at us were gone. I assumed their disappearance was a courtesy to allow us the comfort of privacy while we arranged our places, but I learned later that they had done so from shyness and fear of me. The stale smells of tobacco, of decay, dead fires and damp bodies were heavy and specifically recognizable. The walls of the long room were also of bark, the roof of sago leaves. I stepped on the uneven bark of the floor and it crackled underfoot. Mats of sago spathe, shiny and black with body oils, surrounded the fireplaces.

Kas sat down and cried out, "Ow!" and quickly rolled onto his side. I saw a mass of running sores on his buttocks. How had I missed them? In the canoe he was always in front of me, too far forward for me to see his lower back because of the three paddlers between us. In the bivouac it had been too dark. He had not complained. He stretched out face down and I looked at the pustules and said in disgust, "Why didn't you go to the hospital in Agats?" I spoke no Asmat and my Indonesian wasn't much better. Kas spoke only a few words of Indonesian but it was enough for him to recognize the words *rumah sakit* as meaning hospital. With a word or two and with some gestures, we had little difficulty understanding one another.

"Rupiah tidak ada," he said. "There is no money." I knew that the nurse at the hospital was selling the medications the bishop had donated. They were meant to be given free of charge to the Asmat, who had no source of income, but there was no way of controling the government employee who dispensed the drugs. He would treat no Asmat without payment.

I had not brought along a syringe, but my patrol box contained antibiotics, sulfa salves, and penicillin tablets. I smeared the sulfa over the sores and the pain seemed to disappear immediately, as if Kas believed I had performed magic that cured instantly. I cautioned him not to sit on his buttocks but to lie on his side or stomach and not to wear shorts until the healing had begun. When bamboo tubes of water were brought in, I gave him two tablets of penicillin. The sores healed completely within a week.

It was dark inside the house, even during the brightest part of the day. There were no windows and only one doorway that I could see. It was hot and I was perspiring, though Kas' skin was cool. I sat with my legs straight out, my back against the bark wall, looking up at the storage racks where chunks of sago swarmed with roaches and bundles of clothing were piled with spears and drums and bows and arrows. Kas pulled down one of the bundles, unrolled a ragged shirt and took out a human skull. He ran a hand over the forehead and said his father's name, Sai. He put the skull down on the floor, stretched out, placed the skull under his own head and fell asleep. I tried to sleep, too, but the noises and movement of the floor as people stepped heavily into the room disturbed me. Kas slept on, secure in the knowledge that his father's spirit would always protect him.

The women and children began to arrive late in the afternoon, carrying firewood and fish caught in oval nets in the shallow waters of the Ewta at low tide. They brought in fresh sago and shrimp and catfish and nipa fruit. They stoked the fires with their fingers, picking up the coals and blowing them into flame. Some women brought in embers they had used in the canoes to roast their midday meal and light their leaf-wrapped cigarettes. As they passed by they avoided looking at me. Instead, they glanced my way only when they thought my attention was elsewhere.

Kas woke up just as his two wives had finished cooking. Several men came in carrying their bows and arrows. They slid the weapons into racks and sat down. There were sudden shouts from outside, the footsteps of running men, and the yelping of dogs. Most of the men ran to the doorway.

"*Babi*," said Kas in Indonesian. "*O!*" he repeated in Asmat, pursing his lips and smiling. A wild boar had been killed and was about to be cut up for apportionment beneath the house.

When all the fireplaces were lit, I counted two rows of them, six to a row. The twelve hearths would have meant twelve families had

I not already learned that second and third wives usually had their own places.

Kas and I were at the fireplace of the older of his two wives. The younger one, about eighteen, had two children with her. She had large, round eyes and full cheeks in an almost circular face. Her head had been shaved after the death of a brother, and no stubble had yet appeared to roughen the smooth gleam of her scalp. Mourning strings hung from her neck, covering her chest and back. She wore a cap of interwoven sago leaf folded so that her face could be hidden when outside the house. Tufted bands of twisted fiber had been woven onto her upper arms and wrists, around her upper thighs, just above the knees, and at her calves and ankles. A thicker band was tied tightly around her chest, pulling her full breasts upward. (These signs of mourning disintegrated months later and fell apart.) Her skirt was a belt around the waist to which were tied strips of sago leaf, bunched together under the groin and tied up in back. She also wore stubs of cassowary quills vertically through her nostrils as decoration. One of her children suckled at her breast while she turned balls of sago in the fire. The other child, a girl of two, sat between her thighs until Kas took her for the night and she slept within the folds of his body. The mother slept on her back, the infant face down on her breast.

The older wife, a sister, not in mourning, was decorated differently. She too wore cassowary quills through her nostrils, longer than those of her co-wife. Six oval, mother-of-pearl segments, concave and nippled, from the chambered nautilus shell, were strung together into a necklace. Another necklace hung below it, two human jawbones tired to two long cassowary quills. The jawbones, black with use and storage above the fireplace, were from the heads of enemies; they had been discarded during initiation ceremonies. The jawbones of ancestors, unlike those of enemies, were kept intact and were tied permanently to the skull with rattan strings.

Although Kas' young wife peeked at me from under her cap through half-closed eyes from time to time, the older woman was bolder and, even though frightened at first, came to look directly into my face. She never put food into my hands, however; whatever she cooked for me—the sago and bits of meat and fish—she gave to Kas who passed them on to me. Kas, I found out later, paid as much sexual attention to the older woman as to the younger; he might otherwise have received painful blows on the head with a fist or piece of firewood, or he might have been given rotten food. When I asked which of his wives was more beautiful, he said without hesitation, "My first wife. Her sago is best!"

Kas had married two sisters, a common practice in Asmat. Since there was only one men's house in Otsjenep at that time, which was divided in half into two clans by a central fireplace, the sisters came from the half opposite to that of Kas in order to avoid incest. Wives who are sisters usually get along well, unlike unrelated wives, the younger of whom are given a hard time, forced to do most of the heavy work of gathering firewood and pounding sago.

I wrote in my journal several times a day; I put down everything I could remember of the trip from Agats and began taking notes on whatever I saw in the house: the sago bowls of wood and leaf in the racks, the digging sticks, the drums and spears and bows and arrows. I recorded the way the house was constructed, the number of adults and children; I made a plan of the fireplaces, with the names of those who sat and slept there, and I tried to make out how the food was divided, a complex subject I was never able to understand.

The women left each morning after dawn. When they were gone, Kas would get up and take a piece of fresh sago from the rack over the fire, break it in two, and press and mold it into balls which he put into the glowing embers. I soon realized how effective their storage system was; the smoke rising from the fires kept away the roaches and other insects, which attacked only the food in the racks along the eaves. Kas turned the balls of sago with his fingers. When they were black, he broke one apart and handed it to me. I took out my jars of peanut butter and jelly and smeared a gelatinous mess onto the crust. Kas ate with more than his usual gusto.

On my first morning there, when we finished eating Kas went to the far end of the house and came back with two drums. They were intricately carved and were patinated to a deep, shiny black from the hands that had caressed and rubbed and beat them, and from having rested within the drummers' thighs. They were named Yaor and Waika for the elder brothers of Kas who had been killed years earlier in a battle with Pirien, before that section of Otsjenep had broken away and formed a separate entity downstream. The drums were hourglass in shape, about three feet long, with headhunting symbols carved on the body; in high relief, on both, an abstraction of banyan tree roots and the feet of flying foxes; incised, shell nosepiece and scarification designs. A handle projected four or five inches from one side, carved in the round with human figures and the heads of hornbills that represented Kas' brothers and other dead relatives, all specifically named.

I knew almost nothing then of the meaning of symbols or much of anything else for that matter, though I had read whatever was available in English. In this way I knew that Kas, like all Asmat, believes that death comes only through magic or the hand of an enemy, excepting only the deaths of the very young and the very old. All other deaths must be avenged. Spirits demand vengeance before they will leave the land of the living for Safan, land of the dead, somewhere in the west. Carvings and other artifacts are named to remind the living of their obligations. Even today, almost everything they turn their hands to, from dugout canoes to paddles, from shields to spears and sago bowls and bows and arrows, are named for someone who has recently died. These artifacts of daily life embody the spirits of those for whom they are named, and their presence gives warmth and comfort to their owners.

The deaths of Kas' brothers had long since been avenged and he could therefore, almost with impunity, give the drums in exchange for whatever he needed or wanted: a steel axe, a parang [machete], several sizes of fishhooks, six rolls of nylon fishing line, matches, razor blades, and the inevitable lempeng, a plug of the spiced, pressed tobacco to which the Asmat are addicted. These drums were the first carvings I collected in Asmat. I did not think of the museum; I thought only of my personal relationship with them and felt they were mine. I rubbed my hands over the smooth surfaces and had visions that immediately skittered through my head of stabbings and decapitations, of wild feasts and dancing men and women, of the sounds of yelping, chanting, and drumming.

My sleeping mat was close to the fire. Kas and his daughter were doubled up together just beyond my feet. Older wife was on the other side of the fireplace, snoring lightly, her thin body covered with a torn cloth that might have been a sarong at one time. I could not see the younger wife or any of the others who slept there. One of the drums was my pillow, too hard and high for comfort but I hoped to absorb from it not only the essence of Kas' brother, but his whole life as well. For hours, I tossed this way and that, almost in a doze, always on the verge of sleep but never falling into it. Finally, I took a valium.

Chapter

FIVE

TWO young men were responsible for taking me regularly into the swamp to bathe. I learned years later that they were bond friends, *mbai,* put together to strengthen clan ties by their parents when they were just beginning to walk. Kas had seen me washing in the mud and salt water near the house and had told Kokorai and Amer to take me to sweeter water. They were in their mid-teens, slender, without the powerful arms, shoulders, and chest muscles they would develop within a few years from paddling every day. They were always in good humor, full of laughter and amusing anecdotes and information. Our first time out together, we passed a couple lying in a dugout. Kokorai said, "Oh! You must watch out for that! Remember that if you are out in the jungle and come across a couple having sexual intercourse, you must jump right over them. Don't go around trying to hide yourself. Jump right over them and yell at the top of your lungs, yell out your own name. Then they will have to name the baby after you. If they don't the baby will sicken and die."

Voluptuously, we bathed amidst huge yellow water lilies in swamp water black yet clear. The boys had never seen soap before and luxuriated in lathering themselves. They soaped their bodies again and again, using up most of a bar each time we went out. They enjoyed the sensuality of it and always immediately showed erections. Not at all put off by my presence, Kokorai leaned onto the bent back of Amer, pushed his penis into him and pumped away enthusiastically. Within a few minutes, they reversed roles.

The details of the relationship between bond friends in parts of Asmat had been unknown to outsiders. That this one aspect was

42

revealed to me so easily and so directly spoke of something about me that the men recognized, some overt gesture on my part, some restlessness seen in my eyes or filtering through my skin. The missionary of the region was on leave then, and sexual solace pervaded the villages in which he preached, though the jungle had always been reserved for what the people thought of as their normal lives since the arrival of the mission. In acting out their desires so spontaneously with me looking on, Amer and Kokorai demonstrated that they knew I was sympathetic, possibly a participator.

The intimacy between Amer and Kokorai was the first tangible evidence of the behavior that I had expected to find in Asmat, and it gave me a sense of acceptance. I no longer felt isolated, as I inevitably felt under Western concepts that denounced such practices. I had entered into them, had been part of them, in Peru, Thailand, Mexico, Japan, Korea, Uganda, Kenya, and elsewhere. It was as if homosexual relations existed everywhere, even though, more often than not, they might be underground.

It was in Asmat, however, that I felt for the first time part of a universal clan, for Asmat culture in some regions not only allowed for sexual relationships between men but demanded that no male be without his male companion, no matter how many wives he had or how many women he might be sleeping with. Who can know what it meant to me to find myself in a group where I was no different from others in that one way?

Why did I have to go out of my country, out of my culture, out of my family, to find the kind of assurance and companionship necessary to my inner peace? Why did no one tell me early on that I was not alone? Why was I always guilty? What can heterosexual men and women know of what it is like to be homosexual—the suffering and frustration of always hiding a vital part of one's being? Which of them knows what it is to be always furtive? Not for an instant would I deny the deep understanding, the love, the open-mindedness, the tolerance, sympathy, empathy, compassion of my close heterosexual friends. They are essential to my life; I rejoice in them and love them. But they do not know that particular form of deception and pain, what it is always to be on guard, always to be afraid of being laughed at, sneered at, hated, repelling people, angering people. It doesn't matter that attitudes sometimes appear to be in change; what matters is that I raised myself to relate to that intolerance and have lived my life as an undesirable. Even in my openness to the understanding of my friends, that understanding is never complete; just as I can never understand completely what it is to be a woman, to be heterosexual, black, a Chinese, a Hindu, or an Asmat, they can never come to a complete understanding of what it is to be homosexual. But then, what love or friendship *is* complete in that sense?

"If by chance," said Kokorai later, "you are in the jungle and you come across a cassowary egg, do not pick it up. First, you must run away, swatting at your ears and your head as if bees were chasing you. Only then can you go back and pick up the egg. If you don't do this, the egg will surely be spoiled."

We were in the canoe when Amer pointed to the bank of the river, where a huge black bird stood, a cassowary, in fact, oblivious of us. I quickly took up my camera and held it in front of me. I snapped photo after photo, the clicking of the shutter making no sound that disturbed the four-and-a-half-foot creature. Suddenly, it was no longer there and I realized that I had not seen it with my eyes, only through the lens of the camera. I was furious with myself and with the camera. I was angrier still, months later, when I learned that in my haste to take the pictures, I had used the wrong exposure and ASA.

In my ignorance of the area, I did not know that the place I was visiting was only a small part, the Kamur section, of the village of Otsjenep. I learned this when I was prompted to move on by the smells of putrefying flesh and the wailing of women. An old man died, his death announced in the middle of the night by the moaning, crying, wailing women of his fireplace. I had not known the man was ill until that moment, although it turned out he had been suffering from chills and fever for some time. Had he died suddenly or been killed in battle instead of after a prolonged illness, the family would have sat around the body, while the head of the family asked questions of the corpse. I saw this the following year in my friend Akatpitsjin's village when a man called Waikar died. His body was placed on a mat on the floor, its head leaning on the thigh of Omah, a brother-in-law. A dozen other men sat in a semi-circle facing him. Isimi, head of the family, Waikar's father's brother, took up his spear and touched Waikar's forehead with its cassowary claw tip, asking of the dead body, "Who killed you? Did your killer come from the village of Basim? Did he come from Japtambor? Did he come from Santambor?" Isimi waited several seconds between questions for some reaction from the dead Waikar, but there was none. Soon Isimi had named all the nearby villages, without response. Isimi then proceeded to ask about each house in the village. "Was it the house of Sai that killed you? Was it the house of Kuit?" Had the body indicated that the killer came from one of those particular houses, each person in the house would then have been named. Isimi changed to a different tack, questioning Waikar whether he had by chance eaten a food that was taboo for him. Finally, he asked, "Did you eat the *sasor* crab, which you knew you should not eat?" The body almost jumped up from the floor, frightening us all. I did not see Isimi push or shove the body and do not know how the movement came about. The men knocked their spears together and gave a single great shout in unison, "Whuh!" Everyone ran to the river screaming out, "It's all right! Don't worry! He died from eating the *sasor* crab!"

In Otsjenep, the women closest to the dead man climbed down the ladder, threw off their skirts, threw themselves naked into the mud and rolled around. The mud, almost white when dry on their dark skin, hid the smells of their bodies from the evil spirits that might be lying in wait.

In the morning, the men of the family built a platform of sticks and set it on poles about seven feet above the ground. The body was carried down from the house, washed with clear water, wrapped in a mat of pandanus leaves, and laid out on the platform. The women stamped their feet, held onto the poles, and walked slowly with bent backs around the platform. They cried out and wailed and rolled again through the mud. The mourning and chanting went on for weeks, though I did not stay to watch or listen.

A few days after the death, when the body had outwardly begun to decompose and the smell sickened me, I decided the time had come to leave. Corpses rot quickly in the humidity and high temperatures of Asmat. The putrid fumes rising from what was left of the old man attracted dogs and other animals. To protect the body against scavengers, boys and young men were delegated to watch over it. The flesh must decay naturally, the resulting maggots a natural part of the whole life process.

Soon after I left for the downstream sections of the village, I returned to visit Kas and saw a relative of the dead man cut pieces of flesh from the thigh and pack them around the muscles of the back of the head. Kas made me understand that those connective tendons and muscles are the toughest in the body and take the longest to break down. By placing the meat of the thigh's quicker-rotting flesh around the neck, the process of decay was speeded up.

The family was waiting for the skull, which could not be taken from the skeleton until it separated from the spinal cord of its own accord. Hence the packing of the flesh at the back of the neck. Once disconnected from the first vertebra, the skull would be inherited by the oldest offspring, in this case a daughter. The family would revere the skull, wear it, sleep on it, decorate it, store it away and take it out for special feasts or times of evil in the land. The spirit of the dead man would always protect them.

The clean white skull would later be decorated, the eye sockets and nose hole filled with beeswax and coix and abrus, the coix or Job's tear seeds pale gray or pale blue grains that sprout from a grass like wheat, the abrus a vine of the pea family that produces a pod with red seeds. The jawbone would be tied in place with rattan and the top of the skull covered with a net decorated with feathers and rows of coix. The bones of the skeleton would be wrapped in leaves and taken upstream to be placed within the roots of a banyan tree where benign and righteous spirits dwell.

These death rituals began to change in Otsjenep during a cholera epidemic in 1962, when Father van de Wouw, a missionary of the Sacred Heart under Bishop Sowada, tried to do away with the 120 dead bodies that were laid out on platforms in front of the village houses. The smell of decaying flesh was so overpowering that he could barely keep from vomiting. He tried burying some of the dead but the mud would not hold them; their arms and legs and other parts popped up at high tide and dogs walked around with pieces of the bodies in their mouths. Van de Wouw sat all through one night with the village chiefs, trying to decide what should be done. He insisted that if the bodies were not properly destroyed, more and more people would die. When no solution was forthcoming by morning, he suggested burning the dead, at which the chiefs cried out in horror. Burning of the dead was forbidden by the Asmat because the bones turned to ash, thereby doing away with the spirit as well as the flesh. However, everyone was trying to stop the dying. The chiefs went out to talk to the people. When they returned they said that if Pastor thought burning was the only way to stop the deaths, the people would agree, though Pastor would have to light all the fires himself.

A nurse who was working with van de Wouw at the time said she heard people plotting to kill him if he burned the dead. Undaunted, van de Wouw went out, splashed the 120 bodies with kerosene, and lit them one by one with his cigarette lighter. This was the only way all the bodies could be burned in one day. They burned in such a way that the corpses fell apart and van de Wouw had to watch carefully to see that pieces did not fall into the river, contaminating it. All through that terrifying day, the nurse complained that the pastor would be killed if he did not run away. By nightfall, the village was black with smoke. The sounds of wailing could be heard for miles around. A great shout went up at one point, frightening van de Wouw, who thought his time had come, that the people were preparing to kill him. Resistance would have been pointless. Instead, the people were crying out that the plague was over, that there would be no more deaths. Since then most villages bury their dead in cemeteries in the jungle.

Chapter

SIX

KOKORAI and Amer, always ready to travel anywhere, took me in a canoe through grasses toward the main section of Otsjenep. We stood and paddled, though I, for one, had not yet learned to balance myself properly. I was more than a head taller than either of them, an admirable attribute in itself in their eyes. Standing between them, even with my obtrusive white body contrasting so sharply with the deep sienna of theirs, I was as happy as ever in my life, and I felt part of everyone and everything around. The sun sparkled on beads of sweat on their faces, backs and chests. The night before, their black bodies had shone with purple; in the daylight the highlights were almost red. Their skin tone changed continuously. We paddled while herons and egrets flew up around us. The boys sang and I sang with them:

> *Sisi ya,*
> *yuwa sisi ya.*
>
> There are shrimp
> in the little river, there are shrimp.

Soon I heard drumming, a monotonous unchanging beat to which we adjusted the rhythm of our stroke. From the mass of green of the forest, startling red and black and white appeared, shocking me for the moment it took to understand a shield was there in front of us, held by unseen hands. The grasses parted and a canoe moved toward us, the men hidden behind the shield but the paddles all visible, moving in unison on one side. The effect of

48

the shield's designs emerging from the reed almost made me lose my balance.

The drum in the canoe gave off a constant beat. With the grasses enveloping the dugout, it was impossible to see how many paddlers were there. "Whuh!" grunted eight or nine or ten of them. "Whuh!" they grunted again. "Whuh! Whuh! Whuh!" And then came the sound of their paddles clacking against the side of the canoe, clacking inside me too, and echoing there.

The canoe disappeared into the grasses, turned around, reappeared and led the way. The men had known I was coming; someone had gone from Kas's house with the news of my departure and a group had come to escort me.

I was still paddling with Kokorai and Amer. Two men joined us from the other canoe and those gutturals began again. With each stroke, we all grunted, "Whuh! Whuh! Whuh!" The men danced, wiggling their knees in and out. The canoe bounced up and down. There was a pause, the paddles were lifted out of the water, and the men let out a vowel sound that chilled my bones: "E-é-é-é-é-é-é." The repetition went on, "E-é-é-é-é-é-é-é-é-é!"

The grunting began again as the paddling continued, "Whuh! Whuh! Whuh!" There is no way to describe this sound that reverberated throughout my body.

Without warning, the men's house rose up in front of me. A cloud of smoke seeping through the roof obscured the scene but I could see men dancing on the porch to the beat of four drummers among them. The water of the Ewta was so high we were able to paddle to the ladder of the men's house itself. We climbed and entered.

Inside the smoke-filled *jeu,* the noise was ear-splitting. The room itself, easily seventy feet long, shook with the crowd of dancing men. They yelped and wiggled, each man dancing for himself alone, each one laughing and jerking his hips in a way that slapped his genitals up against his abdomen. Perspiration poured down their bodies, flew around the room, glistened on their chests and arms and thighs and ran down their calves. In the dim light the fires cast a glow that flickered everywhere. The drumming was accompanied by songs of headhunting, of the war between Ots-jenep and Pirien, of other battles, of bravery and love and of the dead whose spirits had been avenged and of those still awaiting the time they could go on to Safan.

I had seen no women. None had appeared when the canoe arrived and none entered the men's house. It was when food was suddenly being passed that I saw wives and sisters and daughters at the doorways, handing in sago and catfish and crustaceans. None were allowed to enter. Young children sat with their fathers and often got up to dance but no females over the age of five were to be seen inside.

On the edges of the shuffling, quivering, jubilant throng of men, small groups worked on war shields. They sat at the sides of the *jeu,* close to the walls, next to the doorways. Six or seven men in a group held the shield across their laps as they refined the relief work on the surface with a small nail chisel, directed by the master carver. In the midst of the dancing men, they concentrated on their work as if they were alone in the vast room. In their intensity, they reminded me of Orthodox Jews around a small table, hovering over the Talmud.

Weeks earlier, when it was announced by the elders that a shield feast would take place, the better carvers were asked to make shields by villagers who wanted memorials of recently dead relatives. Each of the carvers had gone into the jungle and brought back one of the buttress roots of a rhizophore, a mangrove tree, and had begun work. At the same time, other men and women of the village had gone into the jungle to cut down hundreds of sago trees for the grubs of the capricorn beetles that would mature six weeks later in holes the men made in the tree trunks. In these holes, the beetles would lay eggs that produced the larvae, eaten raw or roasted on coals, that are essential to every feast in Asmat.

When I entered the *jeu,* the master carvers had already done their work. The groups with shields in their laps were relatives of the man who had ordered the shield. The family participated only in the final preparations, working on the last subtleties of the reliefs so that they themselves had a feeling of fulfillment and ownership. I could see an intensity in the owner as he worked, a state of mind so powerful that he might easily come to believe that he himself had carved the shield. This became evident as I collected more and more artifacts and the difference between owner and carver was obscured with time.

When it was dark outside the men stopped work, put the shields to one side and covered them with sago leaves lest the spirits desert them before they were properly named. Some men went home to their families but most remained in the *jeu*. The drumming and dancing continued through the night, increasing in frenzy toward dawn until the men slowed down, stopped, stretched out on the floor, and went to sleep. I too slept briefly on my pandanus mat, next to Bawor, master carver.

After morning sago, the men uncovered the shields and brought in carved wooden bowls of powdered pigments: white lime from burnt, crushed mussel shells, red ocher from the earth upstream, black soot from the fire—the only three colors found in that part of Asmat. I sat with Bawor and watched while he supervised the washing on of the pigments, pointing with a finger to the areas to be painted. Each color was mixed with water. The white was washed first over the background surface with a clump of shredded rattan or sago leaf. Before it was dry, the red was painted on inside the outlines of high relief, worked in with a finger or a stick with one end frayed into a brush. Finally, the black was rubbed into the raised outline of each design.

Men, sitting cross-legged nearby, were preparing decorative tassels by rolling sago fronds into thread on their heels or thighs, then tying the thread into small holes along the sides of the shields and around the phallic projection at the top, the penis of the shield. Other men stood alone; still others were dancing, sitting, watching, talking, bringing in sago and various foods. Two men had completely isolated themselves and were carving artifacts that had nothing to do with the feast—a paddle and a sago pounder.

Bawor was a chunky man, broader than most Asmat, solid, compact. Tiny curls of hair covered his chest. On both arms, high up, he wore wide bands of interwoven rattan; on the left arm, he also wore four pairs of pig tusks tied together, a sign that he had taken four heads in battle. Another clue to his prowess was the feathered bag hanging at his chest; less important men wore the bag on their backs. The upper half of his face was brilliant with paint, making it difficult to see his true features. Like the other painted men, he appeared a violent and angry demon. Across his forehead was a streak of white, around his eyes the red of an angry black king cockatoo, while a black line high on his cheekbones made the red strikingly effective. His nose projected far beyond where it might have had he not worn a nosepiece through it most of his life. The hole in his septum was empty at that moment and, as I moved up close, I could see through it into the distance to men walking around the *jeu.* On the back of his head, looped tassels of sago frond were tied into his hair. He knitted his brows and spoke in serious tones as he explained the different designs on the shield.

"*Bipane,*" he said, taking his own shell nosepiece out of his bag. Two pieces of shell had been cut into opposing spirals and had been set together with a lump of beeswax. Bawor took the shell and inserted one of the ends into the hole in his septum. He turned the shell again and again, passing it through the hole until the center was tightly filling his septum. He smiled, unwound the shell, took it out and put it in front of me. With his right fore-finger, he traced the entire outline of this *bipane,* the shell itself, then traced the topmost curled motif on the shield, showing their similarity. It was a design common in Asmat: a headhunting sym-bol, curved like the tusks of the wild boar it was meant to person-ify. The design would terrify the enemy. On the shield, the curls ended in small handlike representations. "*Tarep,*" said Bawor: the foot of a flying fox, a fruit-eating animal like the black king cock-atoo, another headhunting symbol. Bawor pointed to the one other large design on the shield, two connecting spirals, very much like the *bipane* but curving down in the center. "This is *ainor,*" he whispered into my ear. His voice was both proud and full of wonder.

"What is *ainor*?" I asked.

"*Ainor* is *ainor,*" he said, as if everyone knew that. "It is frightening. When your enemy looks at it, he is already dead. When he looks at *ainor* he is so frightened he drops his weapons, his shield, his spear, and his bow and arrows. He cannot run away. He tries to run but he cannot move. He is just there and we take him."

I never found a translation for *ainor*. Wherever I went in the south of Asmat, the description was the same; when confronted by the *ainor* the enemy is always immobilized with terror. He shakes and pants and falls down. His captor can then easily take him into the canoe where he is seated bent over, tied to a crosspiece, with his head down. The canoe stops at the bend of a river, where the whirlpools are, where the spirits dwell, where the enemy will be decapitated.

I did not understand the whole meaning of the design. I asked, "What happens when two enemies with the same *ainor* on their shields meet face to face?" The eyes of the men around turned blank. No one understood the question and no one attempted to answer.

The ancestor for whom the shield is named may give it even greater power than its design. The ancestor's spirit lives in the shield and is a presence that endows the living relative not only with fearlessness and courage in the face of all odds, but also with the omnipotence to overpower the enemy and become the victor.

Important carvers like Bawor are treated with the same respect accorded great headhunters; they sometimes even rival one another in prestige, expressing their power partly through the number of wives they have. All men learn the process of making canoes, simple paddles, digging sticks, bows and arrows, and other tools of daily life. But for more elaborate artifacts such as shields, drums, ancestor poles, figures, and other ritual objects, the best carvers are called upon. They are not paid in the Western sense of payment, but receive food in exchange. The man who asks for an artifact takes on the responsibility of feeding the carver and his family during the carver's working days. Some objects take weeks or months to complete. Bawor, while working on his shield, would not have been able to attend to the needs of his family; he could not have gone out fishing or hunting or been able to take the family to the sago grounds. He who had requested the shield, therefore, brought the sago and other essentials, always searching out special delicacies such as sago worms, choice bits of meat, fruit, and as much tobacco as he could find to keep the carver happy.

These particular shields in Otsjenep were not all made to be used in warfare. They were, for the most part, to be taken to Agats and sold for tobacco and other goods. It surprised me that the men could so easily give up shields that were being named for the dead, but in recent times they had begun to feel that by carving the shields, by naming them, and by holding the feast, they appeased those ancestors who continued to seek vengeance. I saw later that many shields were kept within the village for defense in battle or in individual fights and as safeguards against dangerous spirits. Some were lying on their sides in front of doorways to keep out undesirable demons while the family was not at home.

One morning I was sitting with Bawor in the *jeu,* watching him pierce dog teeth with a bone awl and then string the teeth into a necklace. Suddenly there was a loud shout and everyone jumped up. The men began running around the room and then rushing out the doorways. The previously joyous mood instantly reversed itself; men were pushing one another, stepping over each other, shouting in what might have been fear or anger, all of them trying to get out of the *jeu* as quickly as possible. The uproar startled and frightened me, I thought the men of Pirien were attacking.

A jumble of painted figures brandishing long knives, spears, and arrows burst through the end doorway into the *jeu.* I was paralyzed, but I could see faces roughly smeared with red and white, noses filled with huge spiraling shell, heads sprouting masses of white feathers, the color and flash of the feathers like flushes of attacking cockatoos and eagles. Everything moved so rapidly around me that the blood rushed to my face, confusing me and blurring my vision. They came in full force, the group of raiders, what seemed like hundreds of them, jabbing at the men, screaming at them, striking them with digging sticks, shooting missiles at their backs, their arms, legs, beating them with fists, assaulting all within reach. Everyone was running in all directions, in and out of the house, yelping, yelling obscenities, shrieking. The long, vicious snout of a sawfish was swung against a man's back and blood instantly spurted from the row of tooth marks. Snakes were carried through the house, thrust out and thrown at the men. I shrank into a corner but was quickly surrounded and saw then that it was not the men of Pirien attacking but the women of Otsjenep, laughing and screeching hysterically. They came with knives and poked pointed daggers into my flesh and howled with glee when blood oozed from the wounds on my arms and legs.

As unexpectedly as they had appeared, the women vanished. This was a day on which they were given license to get back at the men for abuses committed against them daily during the past months. The men beat them for not cooking properly, for not having enough sago or fish in the house, for what they insisted was laziness, for what they thought was flirting with other men, for refusing to have sex with a husband's exchange partner, for any number of reasons, real or imagined. It did not matter that the husband might be doing the very things of which he accused his wife. She might fight back but the physical strength of the man was usually beyond her. This therefore was a day when women could take revenge without fear of retaliation and they took fullest advantage of the opportunity. Attack could occur anywhere at any time and it did.

The men calmed down the moment the women were gone. They had swept through the men's house like a whirlwind, creating havoc, but the men laughed and showed each other their deepest wounds, as proud as if the wounds had been incurred in battle. They looked at the blood on me and patted and hugged me, delighted that I had not been neglected.

Minutes later, a man named Fire took me outside, where his wife Jisi stood with a clump of sago in her hand. He touched her nipples, indicating that I was to suckle. They were adopting me, though I could not remember meeting them before. I did not understand whether this was a spontaneous gesture or one that had been planned for days. My adopted family would henceforth be obligated to feed me whenever I was in Otsjenep and I in turn was obligated to bring them gifts. Fire himself was an unappealing man, exceptionally thin and sickly, short in stature, smelling strongly of ringworm, skin peeling from his whole body. His testicles were immense with filariasis—a disease caused by parasites—bloated to five or six times their normal size and hanging halfway down his thigh. Jisi was very pregnant, stouter than most Asmat women and fuller in the breasts, and looked as if she were about to give birth at any moment. She had a pleasing face and was much younger than Fire. Both wore cuscus headbands dangling with bits of nautilus shell and tassels of cassowary feathers. They wore shell nosepieces too, and several necklaces, one of split bamboo on Fire, a sign of a headhunter. From Jisi's nipples sweet milk seeped out, while Fire's nipples erected when he squeezed the flesh for me to take between my lips, for I had to suck his nipples just as I had sucked his wife's. He broke off a small piece of sago and rubbed it across my damp forehead. He ate the crumbs remaining in his hand, thus absorbing part of me through my perspiration. Jisi ate the last crumbs in his hand. He took other sago and rubbed it into my armpits and ate that, too. Jisi then went home, and Fire and I returned to the men's house.

Late in the afternoon the shields were taken out of the *jeu*. They were lined up side by side, leaning against the porch. Even I felt the energy that surged from them. It was as if the shields were alive and the spirits within impatient to strike out in vengeance for past wrongs. Standing there, one next to the other, the brilliant combination of fresh red and black and white made the shields vibrate in the afternoon light, dazzling all with the unlimited strength within them.

The men took up the shields and danced and ran in a circle, apart from the circle the women immediately began forming next to them. The deep mud splattered us and covered everyone with splotches that smeared the paint on our bodies. It streaked down, giving us a macabre, ghostlike look. A canoe appeared, filled with men carrying old shields, and floated exultantly downstream with long bunches of fresh sago frond waving from the shields and spears and the arms and legs of the men—an apparition that in the past would have borne terror into the hearts and bodies of all who saw them. Their yelping and shrieking were fearsome sounds that penetrated everyone's psyche. The men came ashore and joined in the dance. Our perspiration gave off foul odors but they did not bother me. Older men came up to me, rubbed their hands over the sweat of my body, and rubbed it onto themselves. They hugged me and each one rubbed his chest against my chest while I wiped perspiration from them and took it as a gift of strength. At dusk, the dancing stopped. The women disappeared and the men again entered the *jeu*. The drumming began and the men danced until dawn.

SEVEN

IN the past, it was during the darkness before the dawn that the men would have gone out on a raid in search of revenge and for the heads necessary to certain initiation ceremonies. Their passions would have peaked by then through the singing of battle songs and the chanted listings of those killed by great men of the village and those whose deaths were still to be avenged. The women would have egged on the men to great acts of courage and the whole village would have been in a state verging on hysteria. On this occasion, when the feast ended abruptly without climax, the unresolved needs of the men for a truly violent catharsis left them with a listlessness that found only temporary relief in sleep. Some slept through the day and into the following morning, waking only briefly for food. The next day too there was a blank look on their faces that had less to do with the energy so recently expended than with the fact that their minds and bodies had nowhere to channel the emotional and physical violence they had always expressed through warfare and vengeance. The missionaries thought to fill the emptiness with religion, replacing initiation ceremonies with confirmation, the need for vengeance with a dedication toward peace, the anger and violence expelled in games of soccer. But longings for the past showed in the way the men stared into space, sad expressions on their faces, bodies slumped, limp like marionettes needing other forces to move them. Were they envisioning the time they had fought in hand-to-hand battles? Were they feeling weak and lost without the power, the fearlessness that had almost been demanded of them and which they had always demonstrated in battle?

Otsjenep after the feast seemed empty and desolate. Canoes had been slowly loaded with sago pounders, sleeping mats, carrying bags, fishing nets, bows and arrows, spears, bamboo containers, children, wives, husbands, fathers, mothers, sisters, brothers—all had gone into the jungle to fish and pound sago. They would build bivouacs on small streams and remain there for weeks. Food would be found that was rarely eaten in the village because it grew too far to be gathered on forays of one or two days. Life would be easy and relaxed, very much as it had been in the past; there were no government officials or missionaries to see what they were doing. Sexual activity would be spontaneous and frequent. Wives might be exchanged between bond friends and bond friends might have sex together.

I did not know how much I had learned in Otsjenep, how much information I had gathered without asking questions but simply by watching. I did not know then that the people, the men, had allowed me to see certain aspects of their lives that no other outsider had seen. It wasn't until eight years later that I began to put answers together. I was too excited at that time by the variety, the quality, and the numbers of artifacts I had collected to notice much else. The carvings had been labeled and my journal was full of drawings and interpretations of designs. I was more than ready to take it all back to the museum in Agats. My paddlers had been selected by Bawor, men going to town with shields for sale. Two other canoes loaded with carvings accompanied us.

Otsjenep had had little contact with anyone from the outside world except for a few missionaries and travelers and the group that made *The Sky Above, The Mud Below,* a film showing the first foreigners entering the village. The Asmat had been known for their ferocity since the first attempt to land among them in 1770, by two boatloads of Captain Cook's men from the *Endeavor.* Whether the Asmat were greeting or attacking them will never be known, but the magical lime the Asmat tossed into the air looked like smoke and frightened the Westerners who instantly retaliated against what they thought of as an attack with rifle fire. Twenty of Cook's men and an unknown number of Asmat were left for dead at the mouth of what was later called the Cook River, a name that has since reverted to its original Kuti River, a few miles south of Otsjenep.

The whole of the South Casuarina Coast had retained much of its cultural life when I first went down; it remained isolated for a longer period than Northwest Asmat, where the people had first started cutting wood for a Dutch lumber company in 1955. It wasn't until 1979 that Otsjenep and several villages to the south were tempted to cut wood by offers of tobacco, clothes, parangs, steel axes, and even money from Indonesian merchants and officials.

The men went into the forest in groups of six or seven, cut down trees, cut great swathes through the dense growth in order to roll the logs to the closest river, and then floated them down to its mouth. There the logs were pushed along the edge of the Arafura Sea to the mouth of the Betsj River, a difficult and painful journey of three or four days, sometimes longer according to tides and weather. The men sank in mud to their knees and the logs often bogged down; sometimes they were completely lost, swept away by the sea, leaving the men frustrated over their aborted efforts.

Beyond the mouth of the Betsj, a freighter from Taiwan or Korea might be waiting to load the wood that would be taken to Korea or Japan or most likely to Saudi Arabia, where it was used in the building of houses. Those who reached the great ship sometimes received payment of ten or twenty cents per man per log, sometimes no payment at all because the logs were too small or because the seas had been so high for such long periods that the logs could not be moved for months at a time and became infested with insects. It had done no good for Father van de Wouw to warn of these possibilities; the Asmat had thought only of the tobacco and other goods they would receive when the logs were sold. Insufficient payment and repeated mishaps combined with the poor quality of the wood there led them finally to give up. The area was unlike Northwest Asmat where the forests were rich in huge hardwood trees of many varieties, where the Dutch lumber company had established itself two years after Father Gerard Zegwaard built his mission station in Agats.

Zegwaard, A Dutch missionary of the Sacred Heart, founded the first permanent settlement in 1953, after many visits into the region by canoe from his home in Mimika, northwest of Asmat. He built his house and church close to the Asmat village of Sjuru. In my journal, dated July 1, 1978, Jakarta, I wrote: "Got drunk with Father Zegwaard over beer here at the mission house. We finally went to bed when the electricity went off. He talked only of Asmat and how old and lazy he was, too late to do anything with his notes, though he would be happy to have someone else use them. He remains the vigorous man I had met some years earlier, tall, 6' 3", in fact, almost portly, still a handsome man. I showed him several enlarged photographs of Asmat I was taking back to the museum. Looking at them, he began talking about Michael Rockefeller without prompting, insisting that he had been killed by the people of Otsjenep in revenge for the deaths of three war chiefs in their village, murdered by a Dutch official named Lapre. Lapre had executed them in his effort to stop headhunting after the men had gone on a raid and taken many heads. Michael's death seemed logical as Zegwaard told of it, but there was no evidence of any kind to prove it one way or the other. Zegwaard had been interviewed by Milt Machlin of *Argosy* magazine and had given him his views privately, asking Machlin to write nothing of what was said. Machlin, however, wrote and published it all, much to Zegwaard's embarassment. Will that story ever be laid to rest? Even I mention it from time to time."

Later that evening, Zegwaard talked of his early days and how he used to sit in his sling chair, smoking his pipe. "There were no walkways in those days, you know, only mud, and I sat in my chair, like a beach chair, with canvas, you know. An old man used to sit next to me and when I knocked my pipe against a leg of the chair, the old man picked up the tobacco and ashes, patiently took out a leaf and made his little cigarette. He sat with me every day, and every time I knocked the pipe against the chair, he would pick up the bits of tobacco. In Sjuru, too, I would sit in my chair, and the men behind me would talk as if I weren't there, but knowing that I was listening and hearing every word. 'Oh! It is always good to have tobacco,' one would say. Another would pick up the theme and say, 'Tobacco is good and if we had some now we could smoke.' It would go on for hours like this in the men's house and finally I would give them some. It was funny to listen to them, thinking they were fooling me into giving them the tobacco, even though they knew I always had some extra and would eventually give it to them."

Before Zegwaard's time, a Dutch official by the name of Felix Maturbongs tried to settle in Asmat, first in a village upstream, then on the coast in a place the people of Sjuru called Akat, the Asmat word for "good," a word later corrupted into its present name, Agats. Maturbongs found the climate enervating and most problems of the place insurmountable, though he did have some pleasures, for there are many of his descendants bearing his name. He left when the Japanese invaded Mimika in 1942.

The former head of the Dutch lumber company came to see me when he was in New York in 1981, during one of the extended periods I was there. He had traced me through the Explorers Club. "I was the one who pacified the people," he presumptuously told me. "I was the one who stopped the feasting and the headhunting. I stopped the people from killing one another so we could get the wood out." I did not tell him that headhunting might still be going on in at least one of the villages formerly under his control but, listening to him then, I thought back to 1975, when Father Jerry Thaar and I were in that area and heard that the men of Sagapu had decimated the village of Bifako on the Wasar River, a few miles north of where we were at that moment.

Jerry was among the first of the Crosiers to invite me on patrol. We had met, as I met all the Catholic missionaries, early on during my first year there, while I was living at the mission in Agats, before I had my own house for my own privacy and the privacy of the Crosiers, too. Jerry's home village then was Komor, on the Unir, one of the great rivers of Asmat. He had his own thirty-five-foot mappi boat, so-called because the first motorized boat the Dutch brought into south New Guinea was used on the Mappi River.

Traveling with Jerry was comparatively easy; with two boatmen we were only four people. On later trips with the bishop there would be at least two other Fathers and three boatmen, plus Manu Lamera, cook and general factotum, making a total of eight of us. The mappi was not an ideal boat in which to make a journey of several weeks with so many people. The motor was in the center, covered with a great square metal box. It vibrated so ferociously and made so much noise that it was difficult to talk without shouting. The three Asmat slept in front of the motor, I normally slept on my mat between the motor and the starboardside bulkhead, so narrow I could not turn over without displacing myself. Manu slept on a bench at the stern, just in front of the metal fireplace attached to the rear. The bishop and the two Fathers slept somewhere between Manu and the motor, so crowded together it was almost impossible to keep the ties of their mosquito nets separated; in the morning, they had to be taken down one by one or the strings would become entangled. There were no such problems traveling with Jerry since the two of us had the whole center and back of the mappi to ourselves.

In Tomor, at the confluence of the Unir and Dumas Rivers, Jerry and I were talking with Dajir, the Asmat Protestant teacher there, when an Indonesian crocodile hunter came up and gave us the news of the Bifako murders. Before we could question him, he turned on the motor of his canoe and fled downstream. Dajir ignored the interruption and went on talking about the problems caused by the wooding, problems the Crosiers had been discussing among themselves for some time and which were, in fact, of deep concern to most missionaries there.

"The people ran away as soon as they heard your motor," he said. "They thought you were the government coming to force them back into the jungle. The people all paddled in different directions so the government could not follow. They are tired of cutting wood and want to be left alone."

Dajir was tall for an Asmat, about five feet ten inches. He had short hair and a short beard. He wore a long-sleeved batik shirt and long trousers, both the grayish-brown of the water in which they were washed, the color of the Unir, which was in sudden spate from a cloudburst upstream. It was carrying with it the dissolving mud of the banks, as well as tree trunks and branches on which small white birds were resting. Dajir did not look Asmat, for his nose had not been pierced and was straight and thin, unlike the noses of most men there, which had been pierced in childhood with the point of an arrow made of nibung palm. With a change of skin color, he could have come from almost any part of the world. He had been born near the coast, in a village that had stopped the practice of nose-piercing soon after the missionaries and catechists had arrived to teach the Asmat their religion. The catechists, brought from Mimika by Zegwaard, had sneered at the nose-piercing, a custom they considered barbaric, carried out only by *orang hutan,* jungle people. At the same time, they encouraged the Asmat in their own tradition of filing their teeth to sharp points.

"My problem is with the children," Dajir went on. "They do not want to come to school. It is not unusual. All Asmat like going into the jungle when they are free. No teachers, no missionaries, no government. It is the way we used to live.

"The schoolboys are in the jungle with their families most of the time. I don't blame them. I did the same thing when I was their age. Our old ways conflict with school hours and with school itself. We would wake up in the morning, go to the bank of the river and dig for our morning meal, for mussels and crabs and shrimp. Now, the young have to be in school and have no time to look for food until afternoon. So they arrive at school hungry and are inattentive in class. The families go into the jungle to cut wood and leave the children to fend for themselves. They are too young to gather anything but shellfish, which isn't enough for them."

We were standing in front of the row of houses that lined the river. They were in poor condition, except for Dajir's. Like most teachers in Asmat, he demanded free labor and gifts of food from the people.

"I beat them when they do not answer my questions properly. I beat them, too, when they stay out for several days or weeks or even months. They want to be with their families and they want to have sago and other foods. I tell the camat, the regional government officer, that there isn't enough food for the children when the families are out cutting wood but he looks at me and says the men must bring in more logs.

"Of course, the girls almost never come to school. They have work to do, fishing, chopping firewood, pounding sago, and helping with the youngest members of the family. The older boys have it easier and can go out in their canoes with nylon and fishhooks and bring back fish, but they are too small to cut down sago trees and, without sago, they are hungry and unhappy. Sometimes the whole village goes into the jungle and I am left alone for weeks and have little to eat myself, although sometimes I go with them."

Dajir needed no prompting. The words poured out as if he had been waiting for just such an audience. His own pastor never visited the village, nor had the camat.

"The camat tells the families that the children must stay home and go to school and that they must leave food for them. Sometimes they do, but the boys eat it up right away because they know the sago will spoil in a week or two. The only other people in the village are the old men and old women and they have no food either. They cannot go out alone and pound sago.

"The people used to stay in the jungle for months. They would fish and hunt and gather food whenever and wherever they felt like it. They would hunt wild boar or cassowary or cuscus, pick *kom* fruit or pandanus or nipa or palm shoots or whatever they suddenly decided they wanted to do. They simply went out and did it. Now, when the government makes them stay in the jungle, the old ways are no longer possible."

"He's right," said Jerry. "The government doesn't want to listen to the problems or even acknowledge their existence. When the people are out cutting wood for a long time, they cannot get the foods they need to keep themselves healthy, even though they were never aware of doing so. Somehow, their bodies automatically told them what they needed to eat."

"I know what you mean," I interrupted. "Years ago, I worked in Alaska as a radar mechanic at Elmendorf Air Force Base. During the orientation course, the instructor described the cold winters and said we could believe it or not but we would all suddenly develop a craving for chocolate, that our bodies in the icy climate would instinctively demand sugar and its energy. Sure enough, a few weeks later, I was buying two or three bars of chocolate a day, something I had never done anywhere else."

"Yeah," Jerry agreed. "That's it. Cutting wood means staying in one place for such a long time, making it impossible to hunt or gather what the people normally would be eating. Of course, they don't understand about vitamins or proteins. They are happy when their stomachs are full. Their diet has always been delicately balanced, which accounts for the seminomadic way they used to live, periodically moving from one sago field to another as each was exhausted and gathering whatever foodstuffs were close by. There was never any control on their movements except for the boundaries set by their enemies or the limits of their own inherited sections of the forest. Crossing borders is one of the main reasons for warfare. You know, there is a greater variety of food here than you would think when you look around. Not only the obvious nipa and pandanus fruits but so many others as well. Jackfruit grows wild up here and there are taro [a starchy root] and bananas. There are river birds, parrots, wild chickens, owls; there are crocodiles, several kinds of marsupials and edible insects, bird's eggs, snails, termites, honey, larvae, lizards, rats, and flying foxes. There are wild pigs and wild yams and foods we know nothing about."

I knew that the Asmat did not go out for these foods every day but only as the spirit moved them or when they happened to be in the right place at the right time for ripening fruit or saw some other delicacy. Maybe it is only boredom with specific foods that makes them search out the edibles they need to survive, but they have always supplemented carbohydrates and proteins with enough other nutrients to keep themselves in reasonably good health.

"When they are cutting wood," Jerry went on, "they eat sago and fish and almost nothing else for two, three, maybe four months at a time. That isn't enough variety to keep them in good physical condition.

"Of course, in the jungle there are the inevitable deaths from old age and illness or accidents from falling trees, someone breaking an arm or leg. That's normal. But a couple of months ago, I heard Dajir's Pastor Fraser say that many more people are dying in the jungle since the wooding started. They vomit and shit and we don't have the medicine to cure whatever it is. It isn't cholera, though the symptoms seem the same. The biggest problem is a new one, beriberi, with pain in the toes and fingers and all the extremities, where the flesh doesn't bounce back when you press on it. We've never had it here before. It comes from a lack of Vitamin B1 and makes the people so weak they cannot fight off whatever other diseases come along. With malaria endemic here, the combination of the two is almost always fatal. Filariasis or elephantiasis, whatever you want to call it, is also endemic, you know, where the scrotum or legs bloat up."

We were walking along the river bank, on the way back to the mappi. "Dajir says the population in Tomor is now only a little over a hundred. A big change from when I took a census a couple of years ago of over two hundred.

"In the past, headhunting and warfare and epidemics of cholera and dysentery did away with quite a lot of people. Yet the population remained stable. Now, in spite of the headhunting no longer going on and some medicines like cholorquin for malaria being brought in, the arrival of foreigners has meant a decrease in the population in this area. I know that the south coast has an increasing population but there is no wood down there and the people aren't being forced to stay in the jungle cutting logs."

Dajir came aboard the mappi for a lunch of spam, baked beans, and canned fruit cocktail. The conversation had shifted by then. "It was only a few days ago," he whispered and looked around to make sure no one was listening, "that the headless body was seen floating downstream." It sounded like he was about to tell of the murders of the people of Bifako. "Some man from Jeniseko, way up the Unir, probably killed with a bone dagger by the husband of the woman with whom he was having an affair. The husband would have tossed the body into the river. Then, someone from

Tomor must have pulled it out and cut off the head before throwing back the remains. It was seen a couple of times here and, hours later, down in Munu and, still later, in Komor where everyone assumed the head had been taken from the body in a raid." Whoever had removed the head, whether in Tomor or not, would have prepared it in Asmat's prescribed way and would later have displayed it hanging from his neck as proof of his bravery.

I had thought at first that he was talking of Bifako but the story obviously had nothing to do with the killings there. I listened with only half my attention, and was wondering whether or not the subject would come up and, if not, whether it was polite of me to ask questions.

Dajir looked around again and shivered. He pulled his chair closer to ours. He put a finger to his lips in a Western sign of silence. We were alone; Domin and Johannes, our boat boys, had gone off wandering through Tomor looking for food or gossip or sex. "I must tell you what happened upstream." It was easy to see that Dajir was enjoying himself. The gestures of his hands, his darting eyes, the way he shook his head and moved his lips, the way his whole body moved, in fact, were all attitudes of an actor about to deliver his great soliloquy.

"Bifako is gone! Killed by Sagapu! Everyone!" He got up and went to one side of the mappi, looked upstream, looked downstream, went to the other side of the boat and did the same thing, then sat back down again. His sense of timing was perfect.

"Samsu, the crocodile hunter, has already told us." Dajir put one hand on my knee, the other hand on Jerry's knee. "Everyone is dead. They cut off the heads of all the men and all the women and children and ate them all. I know it is true because Bifako is not there any more. There is no village. Everyone on the Wasar River is frightened of Sagapu because they are stronger than anyone else. Even Ti ran into the jungle to hide."

"Let's go, Jerry!" I said. "Let's go see what's happening!"

"Oh!" he said, somewhat taken aback. "Oh, I don't know. Domin and Johannes won't go." He hesitated, then added, "And we don't have enough fuel." He hesitated again, then said, "Anyway, I have to be back for Mass next Sunday."

I was disappointed. It seemed an ideal opportunity to learn about warfare and headhunting first hand, if the story were true. An hour or so later we were on our way downstream, back to Komor and then, for me, on to Agats.

EIGHT

THE disappearance of Bifako stayed with me. Work in the museum was fascinating but my mind was always drifting upstream and would not forget the story until I went back. Months later, Jerry agreed to go as far as possible on his next patrol, as far as the water would allow the mappi before it ran aground or scraped the rocks.

Two hours north of Tomor, we came to bivouacs on both sides of the river: what looked like a great feast house on the right and three or four smaller houses under construction on the left. We stopped and talked with the men. There were no women we could see; they may have been in the jungle or may have hidden themselves from us inside the houses. Later, we heard that this group represented the clans Erok and Piu that had broken away from Sagapu.

We asked about Bifako.

"All gone," they replied. "All dead. All sick and dead."

The men were nervous and sullen. They would not answer questions about the kind of illness that resulted in the death of the people or what had happened to their bodies. We learned only that there was another settlement from Sagapu further upstream. We quickly realized that we had made a mistake by mentioning Bifako so early in our talk, so we went on.

The river was full of debris. We turned around one bend, another bend, then another. The light was almost gone at six when we arrived at Sagapu. We could barely see the ten houses lined up along the bank of the river, obscured not only by the dimness of late evening, but by smoke seeping through the roofs, covering the houses like a single long, low cloud. On the fires inside, suppers of sago and fish would be roasting, perhaps meat, too. The village was now situated at the exact spot indicated on the map made in 1969, though the people had moved several times since then, following the stands of sago in traditional fashion.

Yelping men clacked their paddles against their dugouts, came up to the mappi, entered it and crawled and climbed everywhere. They took us ashore to the small bachelor house where a long string of magical devices hung from the central beam—bunches of blue crown pigeon feathers, pairs of the faded, pale yellow tail feathers of the bird of paradise *apoda-apoda,* several looped skeletons of small snakes, and a row of the jawbones of wild pigs and the bamboo knives used to butcher them.

We sat around the central fireplace, ate sago and shrimp, and passed out tobacco. Much later, we asked about the people of Bifako. "All dead," they said. "We do not know who made the magic that killed them. It must be Ti. They are *orang hutan.* They are jungle people."

"We have heard," Jerry told them, "that it is you men of Sagapu who killed them."

The men wrinkled their brows in anger. "We killed no one! They died of sickness!" They laughed then, their faces revealing nothing more than their words. A year or two later, they would probably admit their guilt and talk proudly of the number of men and women they had slaughtered. It was still too soon; they might be afraid that we would inform the government.

I traded steel axes and knives for shields, a drum, and a paddle with its upper flange filigreed with the heads of black king cockatoos, its blade incised with the design of a butterfly. There were no figure carvings that far upstream.

We left Sagapu at 8:45 in the morning and arrived at the mouth of the Wasar River at 10:15. The river was narrow, its slow-moving current good for traveling, for it meant deep water. Domin and Kaspar, the boat boys, shouted *"Eu! Eu!"* and pointed to the empty, sandy shore on which a crocodile had been sleeping until our approach. They mimed shooting it with bows and arrows. Neither Jerry nor I had been fast enough or sharp enough to see it. At 12:30, the river narrowed further. Two empty canoes floated by, trailing rattan painters that had broken away from where they had been tethered.

The boys shouted again, *"Eu! Eu!"* and we watched two crocodiles slither across the mud, then slip into the water. Further upstream they shouted, *"Biawak!"* at a lizard with its head above the water, swimming directly in front of us and moving at the same speed as if it were pulling us along. It soon disappeared. We saw a turtle, another lizard, and two more crocodiles—more animals in two hours than we had seen since leaving Agats ten days earlier. Hornbills flew from one side of the river to the other, white cockatoos flew up, circled, settled back into the trees as soon as we had gone by; sleeping flying foxes woke and screeched in tiny voices as they fluttered in fear before returning to their sparsely leafed trees. Massive branches and whole trees sailed down with the current.

We watched for where the village of Bifako had been marked on the map and saw nothing. All evidence of its existence was apparently gone. Hidden logs, floating down, struck the mappi and frightened us all with loud bangs. Something heavy struck the boat, tangled with the propeller, stopped the motor. Kaspar steered us toward the shore and tied the boat to a tree. He stripped off his clothes and jumped into the river from the stern. After a minute he surfaced, then went back down again. He went under and resurfaced several times, and finally yelled out, *"Nder momo!"* A few seconds later, a huge branch popped up from the depths of the river, bobbed up and down, and floated silently around a bend. Kaspar climbed back on board, Domin cranked the motor, it started, and we continued upstream.

At 3:30 we saw two men on the right bank jumping up and down on a log that jutted into the water. They yelped and waved their arms. Neither wore clothing of any kind; both had the look of men who had never had contact with outsiders: eyes wide, searching, penetrating, absorbing the new world we represented. They had heard of white men in a big boat and were not frightened; they had heard that we brought trade goods and had no weapons.

The two men ran along the log and got into a canoe, one of them holding high a stalk of bananas and calling out, *"Isap! Isap!"* asking for tobacco in exchange. They tied the canoe to the side of the mappi and climbed onto the bow where Jerry and I were standing with our feet amidst the anchor chain. Both men were shorter than Kaspar and Domin, shorter than the Asmat downstream. The color of their skin was lighter, almost sallow; the shape of their jawline was less square, the chin coming almost to a point; their nostrils were thin, pierced by small sticks, a short stub of bamboo through the septum. The frames of their bodies were slimmer than the Asmat I was used to and completely unlike the bulky, short men of the mountains to the north and east. They held out their arms and pointed upstream. "Kopa!" they said. "Kopa!"—a village not on any map. We arrived three quarters of an hour later, three bends further on.

Two women, their heads hidden by raised arms so we could not see them or their babies, for fear we would cast spells of black magic, beached a small canoe and ran up the high, steep bank into one of the three houses and were not seen again. Men rushed and slid down the bank, jumped and yelped, yodeled, wiggled their knees in and out. Two of the ten or eleven men wore shorts; I wondered where they had come from. We anchored midstream and went ashore in the canoe of the two men who had boarded us. Their canoe was so narrow we could not sit inside and, to us, so precariously balanced that we could not stand. I felt foolish sitting with my buttocks hanging over both sides.

We sat on the bark-covered floor of one of the houses, on mats of sago spathe, and leaned against a bark wall. The sheets of bark snapped under us when we moved. Above our heads, attached to a crossbeam, were clumps of crown pigeon feathers, the jawbones of wild pigs, the skeletons of fish, and several bamboo knives sticking out at various angles. The men huddled close by, preparing their pipes with the tobacco we put out. The pipes were in two sections, a long one of bamboo, eight or nine inches, the other a shorter, thin tube of reed. The bamboo was filled with shredded sago leaf as filter. The tobacco, rolled in a leaf, was stuffed into the end of the reed. The two pieces were held together and closed up by hand. Simple linear designs had been scratched into the bamboo with a rat's tooth but the reed was undecorated. The pipe was passed around and I coughed for several seconds after one deep puff.

Late in the night, after each of the three pipes had been smoked five or six times, we got to the question of Bifako.

"Dead," they said.

"Gone," they said.

"Eaten by Sagapu," they said.

"Mbimawe here will tell you."

Mbimawe, nineteen or twenty years old, had been sitting behind the older men. He moved forward. "Sagapu killed us," he said simply. "All of us. Sagapu did it. Ofak was there too. We saw them cut off the heads of Djorot and his wife and we ran away. Now, I am here. Now, Ofak is with Ti in the jungle. Ti is afraid and the people are hiding in the jungle. Everyone is afraid."

Mbimawe did not seem excited or angry or upset. He was telling what he had seen. He was used to telling the story and he was used to death and killing. His unblinking eyes stared at us almost blankly and I assumed that behind them were thoughts and memories beyond my ken.

I had often listened to the bishop and to government officials who said that headhunting and cannibalism in Asmat no longer existed, even though there were always stories contradicting them, usually with fewer deaths than in Bifako. Nothing further was heard of the people. No army men or police went to investigate for fear of being killed and eaten themselves. It is unlikely that government officials ever heard of Bifako, in fact. Still, descriptions of murder were commonplace until the end of my stay in Asmat.

Trenk came down to Agats in October 1982, with a story that startled and shocked everyone, though it was not surprising to those Indonesians who believed all Asmat were still a primitive, jungle people. Trenk himself by then was looking different. His hair had turned completely white and his waistline had almost doubled in size from the time I first met him in 1973. He seemed to have become more nervous and excitable as the years passed.

Sometimes he was unable to cope with the problems that came his way. His warmth and sympathy for the people were ever-present, but his relationship with his fellow Crosiers and, I must admit, with some Asmat too, became increasingly strained. I began to feel that I could judge the intensity of his difficulties by the number of chocolates he ate and by the size of that waistline; the mental stress on him could easily be marked by his progressively bloating stomach. There was no denying the fact, however, that his story of three small girls from one of his own villages being raped, killed, and eaten, was a true horror story.

Two families from the Manep section of Manep-Simni went into the jungle to fish and gather food. They spent the night in their bivouac. In the morning they went out to pound sago, leaving their three children, aged three, five and six, to play by themselves. This was not unusual and has not been considered dangerous since the days when headhunting was part of daily life. When the families returned to the bivouac that afternoon, the children were nowhere to be found. The families went into the jungle and searched everywhere, calling out the children's names. Nothing was seen or heard. They returned to Manep and called for help. Most of the villagers spent the next several days out looking for the children. There was no sign of them anywhere.

In Agats, astonishing rumors came over the radio from everywhere and every canoe that arrived brought new stories. None of them had anything to do with the truth as it came out later, but at the time the most acceptable theory seemed to be that the men of Ipaer had committed the crimes in retaliation for past killings by the people of Manep. Two months later, Trenk was back with a complete story, or as complete as was likely to come out.

Andreas Mossore, the highly respected head teacher of Manep-Simni, was the one who discovered the truth. He had noticed that tensions between the two halves of the village had been building up for weeks. Fights started several times a day and were never properly resolved. Men screamed at one another at all hours of the day and night, took up arms, shot off arrows, threw spears, calmed down. When Andreas asked his houseboy what was going on, the young man said, "Manep is still angry with Simni because they had not yet paid for the killings."

"Killings?" asked Andreas. "What killings?"

"Why, the killings of the three girls," came the answer.

Andreas asked more questions, probing until he learned the names of six men from the Simni section who had been involved. He called the men to his house and, after a series of denials and many contradictions in their stories, they confessed and told him what had happened.

The six men had left Simni for the jungle in their canoe. They had seen the two families from Manep settling in their bivouac with the three children. The next morning they paddled past the bivouac and saw that the girls were alone. Passe, the leader, said, "Let us take the girls into the jungle and have some fun." The others agreed and they took the girls, who did not protest. In the jungle, all six men had sexual intercourse with each of the three girls. When they had exhausted themselves, they saw that the girls were so weak and in such poor physical condition that it would have been obvious to everyone what had happened and the girls would not hesitate to say who had raped them. Passe said, "Let us kill them and eat them," and they did. When they were done, they buried the remains.

Andreas asked where they had buried the girls and they said they could not remember the exact location. He told them to go out and bring the bodies back. They went into the jungle to look for them, found three skeletons and took them to Andreas, who immediately saw that they were of adults. The men were sent out again, and again they returned with bones that could not have been of the girls. Finally, they brought back three skeletons of the right size.

"Yes," said Andreas. "Now we have the three girls, but who are the other skeletons?"

"Men and women from Manep," they said. "We killed them and ate them too. But that was a long time ago."

The second time I heard Trenk tell this story, I thought back to a time in Brooklyn when I was thirteen or fourteen. I used to walk down to the edge of the Narrows when there were no orders to be delivered at my father's store and I had already done my homework. At high tide, condoms by the hundreds, flushed out from toilets, could be seen floating everywhere while elegant white ships sailed by in midstream. At low tide, the rocky shore was uncovered. Youngsters, male, threw stones at one another or sailed and skipped them over the river's surface. Scrawny Elizabeth was invariably there, too. She wore her hair in Jane Withers fashion but always unkempt, and she always wore the same tattered dress. She may have been ten or eleven. The boys undressed and splashed in the water. They taunted her until she took off her dress. She wore nothing underneath. Naked, she ran in and out of the water, tossed up condoms in handfuls, then ran back to the sea wall, lay down and stretched out. The boys would stand above her, looking down. "Wow!" they said. "Open up your cunt!" they said, all by then with erections. Elizabeth fingered herself and, one by one, the boys knelt down and, in jerks and writhing movements, entered her and exploded. They screamed and egged each other on. Sometimes there were as many as a dozen. I watched on several occasions but never participated.

One afternoon Elizabeth did not appear. I asked where she was. "Oh? Ain't you heard? She died. Yeah, the other day. I guess the boys were a bit too rough on her."

Andreas sent the six men to the police in Agats where they cut grass for three weeks, slept in the makeshift jail without a lock, were given the luxury of rice as well as sago to eat, and were then sent home. Not long after this, we learned that the people of Buet-Kor, upstream from Manep-Simni, had been involved in similar practices, but there were no details before I left Asmat in the spring of 1983. In 1984 I received a letter from one of the missionaries. "What will Christmas be for the villagers of Pau and Warse?" he wrote. "They had a fight on October 21 and one man was killed, opening the possibilities for future revenge and fights? And another village (Ao) just made a raid and ate their victims. We here in Asmat are aware that the same or worse could still happen in any one of our villages, even after thirty years of evangelization."

That same Father wrote again on November 11, 1985, "Christmas this year will have some special aspects. I begin my 'Twelve Days of Christmas' on December 17, traveling eight hours to the farthest village in my parish. The village is called Ao. On my visit there just a few days ago, I discovered 40% of that village of 350 people awaiting their salvation in the form of a cargo cult. A local man had taken the role of their prophet or captain trying to fill his followers with the belief that if they fulfill certain instructions, Jesus will deliver all the worldy goods they need. Just a few days before my visit, however, they were embarrassed and disappointed when certain materials they had hoped for did not come pouring forth from the ground near the gravesite of a former village head-hunting chieftain. I have had contact with this new 'prophet' and hope to continue contact with him and his followers with the hope that through such dialogue they may return to believing in a Jesus who is willing to give them much more than just clothing, tobacco and money."

Chapter

NINE

I was a different person when traveling with the missionaries than I was when traveling alone. Only when alone, when no foreigners were around, could I allow myself the freedom to express my needs and ask questions the Crosiers seemed to avoid. I followed the leader when I was with one of the Fathers and deferred to his wants. I attended church services several times a week when on patrol, thinking that the people would question my absence. The Fathers themselves always said I did not have to attend, but it was obvious that they appreciated my being part of their entourage.

It was my custom to let my mind wander during services. They were boring to me, just as they must have been boring to those who understood no Indonesian, the language of the schools. It depressed me that I was obligated to the missionaries individually, though I liked them. I wanted to be on my own, returning to Agats only when I had amassed enough information and artifacts to proceed with the museum card catalogue. Life was easier when traveling with Jerry or Trenk or the bishop, since everything was done for me and I did not have to think about cooking or schedules or finding paddlers and a canoe. Yet I preferred to be by myself.

When I was new to a village, Trenk explained who I was. "Tobias is a Hebrew," he would say, "of the same tribe as Jesus," a statement that led to confusion since most of the Asmat had been told by Indonesian catechists that it was the Hebrews who had killed Christ and were now all dead. I do not know what they thought of me in such a context, but there was always a murmur that was indecipherable.

Often I thought of my father while I listened to Mass, imagining his horrified reaction. The hand of the Lord was over me at those times and He would surely strike me dead if I uttered a word or conceived a thought that might be considered Christian. I shook with anticipation and sometimes was even on the edge of believing that the hand was about to come down and smash me. It didn't matter how remote from tradition the church and Mass might be: the words "Jesus Christ" spoken aloud should have filled me with loathing, and the cross itself, shining on the altar for all to see, should have affected me with revulsion and pain, just as the sight of it would have dissolved a vampire. Yet I sat and watched.

My father was intolerant. He could never understand that his own prejudices were equal to those of the anti-Semites of whom he complained. A drunken gentile, a thief, a mugger, or murderer inevitably provoked the same response: "What can you expect from a *goy?*" The raids on his village by drunken Poles during the pogroms that forced him to emigrate were never out of his memory. The devastation had become part of his flesh and blood and nothing could lessen the torment. The dead rose up to claim their vengeance from the living, an eye for an eye, a tooth for a tooth, and my father believed it still, though he kept his unkind behavior within the boundaries of the family. The Asmat dead had demanded that same eye for an eye, though the exacting of revenge had become less important in recent times, with outside influence giving the ancestors the peace necessary for them to leave the land of the living for the land of the dead. It did no good to try to explain to my father that not all non-Jews were anti-Semitic, that not all countries were like the Poland of his time. Jews, too, were capable of getting drunk, of robbing and killing, but such events in his eyes took place *only* because of *them;* it was *they* who caused it all. The nights he returned from the wrestling matches and the fights always ended in anger: "Those stinking Negroes! he would say. "They ruined it again for me. It's a *shandah* they are allowed to sit there next to me!"

Poor man, I see him now sitting on the very edge of his chair in the house of some friends of mine in Georgetown, where I had been invited for a weekend. My younger brother had driven my father down from New York to visit my older brother and his family, and they picked me up for the return trip. My friends asked my family in for coffee. Reluctantly, my father entered his first gentile house, charmingly eighteenth century on P Street. He accepted no food or drink but remained like a rock, precariously poised on the edge of a chair, the brink of a cliff, as if terrified that God, seeing him there, would push him over and deal the fatal blow. Later, in the car, he wondered, "How is it that they like you? Don't they know you are Jewish?"

I was closer to Trenk than to the other Crosiers, though I considered them all my friends; yet even when I traveled with him I was never as intimate with the Asmat as when alone. Another's presence inhibited me, partly because, with a missionary in close attendance, I was automatically associated with the church, which meant that I should disapprove of certain rites that the people continued to practice secretly. It was always necessary to disconnect myself from the missionaries before I could become my idiosyncractic self. Alone I was more relaxed and could more easily accustom myself to the life around me and ask the questions to which I needed answers about symbolism, or feasts, or sexual activity. Allo Sosokcemen, chief of Trenk's village of Ajam, even though a former protege and secretary to Trenk, talked to me more openly away from his own people and away from Trenk as well. He would come to my house in Agats and we would sit on the porch in front of the long walkway that led from the mission pier on the Asewetsj, past the two shops, the parish houses, the primary school and the nunnery, ending at the cathedral, where it turned one way to the boarding school, the other way to the monastery and the museum.

It was never a simple task to get answers on sexual matters when the questions pertained to relationships between men. Trust, understanding, and affection had to be established first. I had known Allo eight or nine years before I first sounded him out on the subject. He had always associated me with Trenk, but he also knew that my approach to life was vastly different. He was only twenty-three and more educated than anyone else when he was elected headman of Ajam in 1977. He had been an attractive boy when we met and had turned into a handsome figure of a man, with aquiline nose, a disarming smile, a straight, muscular body, and an intelligence and sensitivity that sometimes gave him problems. He was articulate and read everything that Trenk or anyone else gave him. Too intelligent not to understand what officials wanted of him, he nonetheless vacillated between helping the people and helping himself. Although he had been out of Asmat on leadership training courses through the mission, he had no experience of the world and only later began to understand and recognize bribery when it came his way. Merchants offered transistor radios, an outboard motor, gas, and other amenities not part of Asmat life in Ajam. The gifts were intended to corrupt him into talking the men into cutting wood for the lumber company. He resisted at times, at times gave in, and then resisted again.

Like all Asmat, he was not yet free of the spirit world which inhabited him and in which he lived. Education in government and Catholic schools had not relieved his fear and sense of obligation to the spirits around him. Whenever government officials and merchants were badly exploiting the people of Ajam, a cargo cult arose, a cult that began after some Papuans had seen airplanes land during World War II, loaded with food and objects they learned to need. The movement was usually led by a self-appointed leader who claimed to have had a vision or dream that showed the miraculous way toward material goods for everyone—guns, tobacco, clothing, radios, steel axes and parangs, and canned foods. When a rebellion started in 1980 among the stronger elements of the village, the head teacher, frightened for himself and for the lives of his family, ran to Agats. Allo was certain he would talk to the police and to the military about the rebellion and that troops would be sent to calm the villagers and to search for those who had run off into the jungle. A magical water, a mixture of wild honey, taro root, and tobacco juice, was being brewed to protect all who drank it. No bullets could enter the body of anyone who swallowed it, and enough was being prepared to protect everyone. Fighters from the Free Papua Movement were certain to come with weapons to help in a war against Indonesia.

Allo told me that two young men were destined to be sacrificed, the pieces of their dismembered bodies thrown through a mystical doorway in the jungle. Weapons and material wealth would then fly back from the other side of the doorway to all who stood there. During this period, it was particularly important that the ritual of *papisj*, wife exchange, be performed continuously. The forces that kept the universe intact had become unbalanced, necessitating the constant flow of semen to counteract its unnerving effects. The universe must be returned to its original state of equilibrium and this could come about only through an intense period of sexual activity. All manner of sex was permitted and necessary, including incest. Anyone who did not conform, who did not contribute to the quantity of flowing semen, would be killed by the great snake that crawled through the village smelling everyone's feet. If the feet did not smell in the right way, the snake would swallow that person. When the snake had eaten its fill, it would expel those inside its stomach in a great explosion of dust. The snake would then resume its journey, smelling the feet of all the other villagers.

The various clans held meetings and everyone was prepared to fight and die for freedom. Allo, fearless himself, spoke to the head of the government in Agats over the radio in Trenk's house. "We have talked this over," he said. "We now ask you to send the police and the army. We are ready for you."

The military man said, "Chief, are you asking that we come and fight you? Is it correct that you want war?"

"That is correct," said Allo.

The magical water was passed to everyone and bitter herbs were eaten to heat up the men for battle. It was then that Trenk began questioning the people, asking them one by one if they were ready to die and to allow their children to die. Trenk himself was not prepared for such an event, he told them. The men began to understand that they were passing a death sentence on themselves and on the whole of Ajam. Slowly they dispersed and the rebellion was over.

Our talk was taking place in mid-1982, two years after the fact. I had been in New York when the rebellion occurred, but had learned of it through letters from the bishop and from Trenk. I was back in Asmat for six months, expecting to finish my work on the catalogue within that time. As always, Allo seemed glad to see me, as if I were a means of connecting him with the outer world, as if I were a medium through which he could gain an understanding of life itself, of the Crosiers and the Indonesians, perhaps even an understanding of God. This attitude on his part may have been only in my own mind, for we never discussed such things; he never asked why I was there, never asked anything personal since the time, years earlier, when he learned that I was unmarried and had no children. Nor did he ask why the government beat his people when they would not cut wood or what life was like in Europe or the United States. There was a comfortable awareness of sympathy between us when we sat alone together, even when I asked for answers that embarrassed him. He'd had guilt feelings at having succumbed to the stories of dreams and spirits and the magical element that was to rid Ajam of oppression forever, and he hesitated at first to reveal himself. Soon, however, he opened up so completely that I knew I could go on from the subject of *papisj* to ask about his own sexual behavior and that of the people in general.

Wife exchange, he insisted, was still common. Bond or *papisj* friends exchanged wives on ritual occasions and at times of stress, such as the rebellion. This had always been so in spite of Father Trenkenschuh, whose admonitions had restrained the people only to the extent that *papisj* was practiced in secret. During the rebellion, there had been few families that did not participate. *Papisj* meant that Allo's wife, having agreed to spend the night with her husband's exchange partner, would go to the partner's house in the late afternoon. There she would cook sago and other food for the man who would be her sexual companion for the night, as well as for the rest of his family. In the meantime the exchange partner's wife would have gone to Allo's house, assuming she too had agreed to the arrangement. After the food was eaten, the family would leave the couple alone and would find places to sleep elsewhere, the men in the men's house, the women with other relatives. It was an exciting time. In the morning, with all four partners sexually sated, and satisfied that the proper balance of energy had been reestablished or maintained through the passing of semen, Allo would decorate the woman he was with and his partner would decorate his wife. The women would then return to their homes. This might be the next morning or three days later, depending upon earlier agreements. A child of this union was considered the child of the woman's husband. The circumstances of this ritual act varied and often took place in bivouacs in the jungle.

Papisj had been known to missionaries from the time they first arrived, since the Asmat considered it vital to life and had no reason to hide it. Other varieties of sexual expression were also open until they were denounced from the pulpit as sinful. Sinners were not allowed inside the church by some pastors; others merely refused to allow them to take part in the ritual of the eucharist.

Ajam, before 1983, was the largest village in Asmat, with a population of about two thousand. It was up the Asewetsj, in central Asmat, and was one of the villages in which the ancestor-pole feast took place. Different areas of Asmat had different types of feasts. Little is known of the sexual life of the past or even of what is still being practiced and hidden. Trenk has written of the *imu-mu* ritual, saying that it "implies a strange relationship between an older man and a young boy. The boys in this relationship are called *imu ipitsj* and are subjected to all kinds of dirty jokes and treatment at the hands of the older men. They are made to sit in front of the old men and then the old men are told, 'Here is your wife!' There is a lot of physical familiarity between the boys and these old men—seemingly in the context of play. How far this ritual includes homosexuality has not been established. Informants denied any existence of homosexual relations in the *imu-mu* ritual."

Allo said he knew nothing of the *imu-mu* and had not heard of it. "I have never had sex with a man," he went on. "Others have, but I do not know the details. The word for sexual activity between two boys or between a boy and a man is *faper. Fa* means ass; *per* is to hook together. It is the same word we use for sex between animals because of the way they connect themselves. When families arrange for *papisj* partners in childhood, the boys usually begin having sex together when they are about five; that is, they play with one another's penis. Later, they have sex by pushing the penis into the ass of the other. First, one does it to his friend; then the other gets his turn. There is always balance between them. We use the words *faper ameris*. There are no words for a man or boy who is on top or for the one on bottom. It doesn't happen that one partner takes the same role all the time. Sex between boys and girls usually begins when the boy is capable of ejaculating. He is about thirteen; the girls begin when they are five or six. This sexual act is called *djimatsj*. It takes place in the jungle, not in the house where several families live. It is not right to do it in front of others.

"A man never sucks the penis of another man, except in certain ceremonies during which the sucking is not done to orgasm. Sometimes, there is *faper* between men but after marriage, this does not happen often. Men do not suck the vagina of women, and a woman never sucks the penis of a man unless, for some reason, it is not possible for her to have sex in a normal way. There is no *faper* between men and women, although now, with so many police and military men coming from all over Indonesia, there is no way to know what is happening, even in my own village."

My reading had prepared me for differences in attitudes toward sexual relations between men among some of the peoples of New Guinea. Gilbert Herdt's *Guardians of the Flutes* gave an account of the Sambia who practiced fellatio within the male population, while J. Van Baal's *Dema* discussed sodomy among the Marind. The people of the South Casuarina Coast of Asmat live close to the Marind, as well as the Jaqai and the Awyu, groups that also engaged in ritualized homosexuality and may still do so, although one of the missionaries told me he had stamped out all sexual acts between men among the Marind some years ago. For them, ritualized homosexuality was necessary to the growth of boys into great warriors. Without insemination by an older man through sodomy, youngsters could not become fully masculine. On the other hand, among the Mimika, who border Asmat at the opposite end, on the northwest, sexual activity between men appears to have been rare. It was therefore to be expected that, in the south, there would be considerable sexual activity among men, and a diminution of such contact as one moved north and west toward Mimika. This was, in fact, precisely the information that came to me as I traveled on. Since Ajam was halfway between the two areas, it is not surprising that there was only a moderate amount of homosexual activity there. Allo's information, together with that of others in Ajam, confirmed this. I learned nothing about women. The men denied the existence of any sexual activity between women and laughed at the idea. The few women I was able to ask refused to discuss sexual matters.

Chapter

TEN

NOT long after that first trip up the Unir with Father Jerry Thaar, late in 1975, when we'd learned of the killings in Bifako, I was at the seismological company camp on the Brazza River, at the invitation of Rob van Houten, the manager. "Brazza" is one of those words that stirs up whirlwinds in me, for it thrusts me headlong into headhunting and traditional life. Until the arrival of the seismological company, the whole of the region far upstream had remained isolated but for a few expeditions that made little or no contact with the people. Those who lived there were too frightened by what they saw and heard of outsiders to appear from behind the leaves that hid them, except when their territory was invaded and their property taken. The Brazza River itself begins in the foothills of the Djajawidjaja Mountains, where the people were still fighting at least as late as 1983 with bows and arrows, shields and spears.

Van Houten came to Agats briefly to discuss the effects of drilling for oil on the people and on the swamp. Jerry and I had met him on the Unir and had asked him to come down to talk to the bishop. A couple of weeks later a helicopter appeared without warning over Agats and landed on the walkway in front of the cathedral. The entire population rushed out to meet it. Van Houten brought six cases of Tiger beer, six bottles of Courvoisier, and a refrigerator chest full of steaks from Australia.

"One oil spill would wreck the food supply of the whole area," he said later in the mission recreation room. "Oil would spread over the surface of the swamp as the tides affected the rivers and the water covered the land. It would seep over everything, killing all the fish and all the sago. The company says it sets up preventive measures for such spills but, in practice, it doesn't work out that way."

Shortly after his visit, it happened that the mappi was going from Agats to the seismological company base at Senggo, where the Navaho plane landed on its flight from Port Moresby or Darwin, bringing technicians and workmen and fresh food. One of the Fathers was going there to reestablish contact with a group of Catholics in a predominantly Protestant region, and I was able to go along.

The mappi started up the Asewetsj and wiggled its way through the forest, always keeping to the river on the right until it reached the Siretsj, the source of which is in the snow-covered mountains almost due east of where it empties into the Arafura Sea. The waters of the melting snows start in rivulets and brooks in rocky crags, then plunge down in waterfalls to become the clear streams of the upper Brazza and the three rivers that become the Kolff before flowing into the Siretsj. In this area, the river beds are covered with stones, some smooth enough and shapely enough to be sharpened into axes. Far downstream, the Siretsj bifurcates, dividing itself into two huge rivers that hold two villages like arms. The lower arm, the Betsj, is two miles wide at its mouth. It meets the shallow Arafura Sea with a force that roils the water and mud, making it difficult to cross in small boats. The Asmat avoid the turbulent currents by crossing most often at dead water or by paddling upstream to where the river is calmer. It was while passing the mouth of the Betsj that Michael Rockefeller's catamaran turned over. The Wildeman comes up from the Mappi area in the southeast and joins the Siretsj below where the Brazza flows into it. Shortly after the mappi turned into the Wildeman, we arrived at Senggo, where I was greeted with the news that four Indonesians had been killed upstream from Mascape, as the camp on the Brazza was known.

A few days later I went on board the company boat that came up from Agats and found van Houten at Mascape having dinner, holding forth on the killings. "For Christ's sake!" he said. "The minute they get those guns in their hands, they have to use them! What were they doing, those policemen, anyway? What did they expect? They left the lines to run after a pig and shoot it. Stupid! Of course they were killed! Did they think the people would just let them kill their animals without trying to protect them? It was obvious they were domesticated pigs from the strings through their ears and it wasn't as if the guys were hungry. God knows, there's enough food here and we won't even mention the fact that they were Muslim and forbidden to eat pig meat. No wonder the people are always mad at all of us outsiders."

We were eating at a long table in the dining/recreation room. My plate was piled high with lamb chops (with ketchup), freshly mashed potatoes (with ketchup), fresh corn on the cob (with butter), and fresh string beans (with butter). For dessert, I had a choice of chocolate cake, ice cream, kiwi and passion fruit, oranges, apples, bananas, white grapes, and cherries, all foods I had not seen since my arrival in Asmat.

"Every week there's something going on. These guys drive me up the wall. They hack at the jungle and go straight through anything that might be in the way. I tell them time and time again: Don't destroy the people's fucking houses, Don't destroy the people's fucking gardens. Go around them. Do you think they listen? Oh, no! They think I'm too far away to know what's going on. How could I not know when there's always this kind of trouble?" He put an affectionate arm on the shoulder of a young, handsome, curly-haired Bulgarian, a recent emigrant to Australia. "Now Kolcha here, he can show you what I mean. He works the lines and is the best man I have. No problems. You go out with him and see what's going on. He'll show you."

The Westerners in the camp, their alcohol, their marijuana, their cutthroat games of Monopoly and darts, the food and the comforts of the tiny screened-in billy-huts, all quickly palled on me. Van Houten gave me complete freedom to travel as I chose, to take the outboard with or without driver or to go out on the lines in the helicopter. I took advantage of the offer a few days after my arrival. I ate a breakfast of scrambled eggs, bacon, french fries, coffee, and Danish, gathered my gear together, stored food and trade goods in the outboard, had the gas tanks filled, and set off alone in search of the people of the Brazza who had killed the four Indonesians. I felt liberated, as if I were sailing through the sky, swept on by currents directed by Fates who knew what I was looking for.

There had been no rain for two days and the river was low, the bank thirty-five or forty feet above the sluggish brown water. It was calm, a hundred feet wide but straight ahead only for short distances, for the river bent and turned around sandy banks or ornamental grasses. It would rain later that night, not heavily, but a downpour in the mountains to the northeast would abruptly raise the level of the river, forcing the water violently downstream, taking mud and debris with it, keeping me to the house I'd come upon in the jungle. The whole character of the forest had changed from that of the coast and all mangrove and nipa were long since gone. Occasional gardens sprouted banana trees and taro grew along the river bank. I was naked in the outboard, comfortable and contained without clothes. I had learned in Peru, living with men who wore only paint on their bodies, that acceptance by them was quicker, simpler, when I had freed my own body and mind of its outer layers, and at the same time, could demonstrate instantly that I was unarmed and vulnerable.

Two hours upstream from the camp, just beyond a patch of small banana trees, I could make out the figure of a man or boy and maneuvered the boat toward him. He was a youngster no more than sixteen, standing beside a low structure of thin sticks and bark, a pup tent of local materials. He was the first of the untouched people of the Brazza I saw and I was dazzled by the look on his face and the ornaments in his nose. He did not look very different from the men of the upper Unir, but there was a wilder, more enigmatic glare in his eyes. Despite his youth there was an arrogance in the way he stood above me, chest out, bow and arrows in hand. He was taking no chances. I could see caution and anxiety there too, and knew that he was not about to trust me. He was also shy and frightened, and opened his mouth as if to speak but said nothing. I wondered what had prompted him to be so daring as to stand there alone before me but I never learned why he had been so open. Later experience proved that first contact was a slow and difficult procedure.

I soon learned that his name was Yoshigipi. A short length of decorated bamboo went through his septum. From his nostrils, the long thin wing bones of a flying fox curved upward in front of his eyes. He wore nothing but the ornaments on his body, a fresh green leaf tied over the foreskin of his penis, a waistband of nine loops of rattan, and a necklace of twisted strands of yellow wire, the cap wire used by the seismological company to set off dynamite. He was covered from the neck down with the circular patterns of ringworm, one of the tineas, the skin flaking off everywhere but from his clear face. When I reached up and offered a lempeng of spiced tobacco, he smiled and jumped down into the mud at the water's edge. He sank to his knees and easily pulled his legs out of the ooze, took the tobacco hesitantly from my hand and tied my boat to the log to which his own dugout was tied. We climbed the bank, sinking deeply with each step.

There were four rough shelters on level ground, all about ten feet long, three feet high at the peak. Smoke seeped through the thatch of each one. I walked toward one and heard a shout from Yoshigipi cautioning me not to approach it, a hut occupied by girls, I found out later. Yoshigipi crawled into the hut closest to the river and I knelt to look inside. Behind a small fire sat two boys about five huddled together with their arms stiffly around one another. Their noses dripped mucous into their open mouths. Their eyes were wide with terror and they screeched at the sight of me, crawled out as fast as they could, and ran into the jungle.

Yoshigipi took his net carrying bag from its support under the angled roof, put the tobacco inside together with leaves for cigarette paper, some small chunks of sago, two small bone tools, and the skull of a bandicoot. We went back down to the river where he loosened the rattan line of his canoe, tied it to the back of the outboard, and climbed inside. He ran his hands over the metal and knocked it with his knuckles, then bent to lick and smell it. At his direction, I took us three or four minutes upstream to another clearing, a great open space where a hundred trees had been felled with stone axes, the stumps still there, the logs still there. The area was deeper than it was wide, reaching back over a thousand feet from the river to the far wall of the forest where a huge house sat high in the trees.

Yoshigipi quickly climbed the bank and began running ahead of me over the branches and logs that were the roadway to the house. He turned to look back and stopped when he saw how slowly and carefully I stepped along the logs that to my sneakered feet felt no thicker than a tightrope, while I balanced my patrol box on my shoulder. He took the case and set it down, emptied his carrying bag, stretched it to accomodate the box, tossed his own articles on top and carried it on his back with the bag's strap across his forehead.

The house was well over thirty feet above the ground, built on poles with one immense tree trunk in the center, very much like the two tree houses of Otsjenep, but much larger and superior in construction, as if built as a permanent habitation. A ladder led the way up at an angle from under the house to the right end, where there was a porch so narrow I was inside in one step. Another platform extended at the upstream end, used by the men of the house as a place from which they urinated during the day and defecated at night. Bending low, we entered through the downstream doorway, used exclusively by men. Another doorway, rarely used during my time there and then only by women, was at the other end of the porch. Normally, women entered from the back on a long, notched log that led to the ground, an easier way up when carrying babies, firewood, sago or other materials and food.

Two women suckling infants screamed when I entered, got up, and disappeared. Yoshigipi laughed. There was no one else inside the house that I could see. Light came from openings between the irregularly spaced logs of the floor and from between the sections of bark that made the walls. It was arranged so that the houseposts down the center divided the long room in half, separating men from women. No one crossed that line, either during the day or during the night. Sexual activity, I later learned, took place in the jungle. There were nine fireplaces between the posts, another eight on the side opposite, close up against the far wall.

Human skulls, blackened with soot, hung from the crosspieces of racks above the fireplaces, while the racks themselves held sago, firewood, skulls of small animals, and the skeletons of snakes and fish. Dogs slept close to fireplaces.

Yoshigipi sat beside me, and with the heel of his hand against his inner thigh kneaded a leaf until it was properly softened, then rolled tobacco in it. He lit his cigarette with a piece of wood from one of the fireplaces.

A man came to the doorway, looked inside, then left. Other men appeared, breathing heavily as if they had been running in their haste to see me. They sat down, touched me, ran their hands delicately over the skin of my arms and chest, examined the palms of my hands and even seemed to count my fingers and toes. If anyone noticed that I was circumcised, he made no obvious comment. The men talked to me as if I understood every word. They all wore decorations in their noses, bone, wooden pins, bamboo, the wing bones of flying foxes. Long twisted strands of the fiber of sago palms were tied into their hair and they wore bamboo ear plugs that held the dried moss or shredded fiber that, together with the loops of rattan they wore as armbands, were used to make fire. Two of the men wore hornbills beaks as penis sheaths, the beaks curving downward from their groins, held in place by a string around the testicles. Most of the men, however, wore a simple, small, fresh leaf covering the head of the penis. Skin diseases and ulcerated sores blotched and spotted the tough bodies of almost everyone and many had filariasis. A pair of adult albino twins looked sickly with their pigmentless skin covered with large red spots, their pale red hair, and the pale pupils of their eyes.

The men laughed, grunted, rubbed their hands over my perspiring chest and back and wiped the perspiration onto their own chests and faces. One old man sat down and hugged me, rolled me over along the floor, interlocking our legs, and pressing our bodies tightly together.

Before long an older man came in. He may have been in his late forties. He had an air of authority that immediately led me to understand that he was the headman. His body was massive and muscular, more so than the other men. On both sides of his groin were the swollen lumps of the early stages of elephantiasis. There were running sores on his thighs and shins. Scars on his chest and back indicated where arrows and spears had pierced his skin. His eyebrows were thick, frowning at me above small eyes surrounded by deep creases. His hair and beard were dense, ringleted, and speckled with bits of leaf and food. He wore no covering on his penis, no decoration of any kind except for a headband of coix seeds. I stood up and he motioned me to sit down again. He stood in front of me, took his penis in both hands and flapped it up and down. The penis was half erect. He moved even closer and flapped it in front of my nose, almost touching it. There was no laughter then; instead, the atmosphere was tense.

I did not know the meaning of this gesture or ritual. An Asmat from downstream might suck the penis as part of certain peace-making ceremonies or when listening to the secrets of a friend, thereby assuring his silence. A Dani from the mountains might touch or hold the pair of testicles in greeting. I was too startled to react except to stare and smile weakly.

No more than a minute or two passed before the headman, De-repen, pulled me up by the hand and threw his arms around me. He had waited to see my reaction and, apparently satisfied, welcomed me as a friend.

The men yelped and the dogs barked. The moment of tension passed as if it had not existed. The men were in good humor and laughter circulated around the room. They cooked and brought me food, first sago from Yoshigipi, then sago from the others, a small piece from each of them. Large shrimp were handed to me, then taro, various fruits of the forest, and a long thin vegetable that grew like corn, was roasted and shucked like corn but looked more like asparagus and had a slightly bitter taste.

Later, on my sleeping mat, with my thin blanket covering me and Yoshigipi, I stared up at the thousands of roaches clustering on a beam and thought about that moment. What had the gesture meant? Why was my reaction acceptable? What would have happened had I shown anger? What would have happened had I opened my mouth and received Derepen's penis? I had visions of myself being forced to fellate the men, one after another. It wasn't until several months later that I began to understand. Carleton Gajdusek has written on the characteristics of primitive man, comparing him with other primates: "The display behavior of the Gothic variety of squirrel monkey in presenting an erect phallus . . . in the case of two males appears to be primarily an aggressive act because it occurs in exerting and establishing dominance. If the recipient does not remain quiet and submissive during the display, it may be viciously assaulted." So that weak smile of mine and my hesitation in deciding what to do had been the correct reaction.

Women came into the house at dusk carrying firewood. They had been made aware of my presence before climbing the ladder. They all wore a simple cache-sex made of bark over the groin. Most of them kept their backs to me and covered the eyes of their children, afraid that I might perform some deadly magic. They sat on the far side of the room unacknowledged by the men. A few missionaries and other travelers had seen men along the Brazza River but no women and children. I do not know why I was permitted inside the house with them; it may be simply that these people were ready for visitors from the outside world, that they knew of the metal tools and tobacco I would be carrying and were hoping for gifts. On the other hand, no girls between the ages of three and thirteen or fourteen ever appeared. The boys and unmarried men who went in and out of the house slept farther downstream, in one of the low huts at which I had met Yoshigipi.

Yoshigipi was assigned my protector and never left my side. He accompanied me everywhere, sometimes to my embarrassment. That first night and on all my ten succeeding nights there, he slept nestled against my back, his penis erect. He was the only unmarried man allowed to spend the night there. I never worried about the contagiousness of his ringworm because I expected my soap to keep my skin clear.

Every morning, accompanied by a group of men and boys, I went to the river and set up my metal mirror, lathered my face, took up my razor and proceeded to shave. This ritual endlessly fascinated them all.

The women and children chewed wild sugar cane that I never saw the men eating. I watched women on occasion drying piles of tobacco leaves. One at a time was placed on a thick section of bamboo, the stem rolled flat with a length of reed, then hung above the fire. Some hours later each woman's fifteen or sixteen leaves were hung in a single batch from a crosspiece in the rafters.

The days went by quickly. I collected shields, smoking pipes, a drum without decoration, and other artifacts for the museum. I could not discover where the shields were kept, a fact that tantalized me. I had only to use the normal Asmat word for shield, djemesj, for the men to hold a prolonged discussion before sending out a group of youngsters. There had been no shields visible in the house. The first time I asked, the young men went out and I waited patiently to see what would happen. Half an hour later they returned with a shield completely different in shape and design from those of the coastal area. My offer of a steel axe and a parang was instantly accepted and the men immediately shouted at the boys to bring another. They reappeared after another half hour with a second shield. They next time it happened I tried to go along, but was not permitted to do so. I never discovered where the shields were kept by any of the groups I visited over the years.

The men never hesitated to trade nose and ear decorations but they had a strong attachment to the necklaces that everyone wore, the wide bands of white pig teeth and the smaller, yellowish teeth of the cuscus. Perhaps, like the jawbones of wild boars strung together and prominently displayed, they too represented the skill of the hunter. And, like the human skulls that magically disappeared when I asked about them, the necklaces vanished when I tried to trade for them. They surely had within them the spirit and strength of the animals themselves.

From odd facts I picked up here and there, I came to the conclusion that it was the men of this house called Kodna who had killed the four Indonesians from the seismological camp: a pair of boots already covered with soot that lay beside the firewood and old crumbs of sago; the bag of one of the men with a piece of cloth sticking out, almost certainly a shirt; and two belts and a cap worn by another of the men. I did not draw attention to any of this and questioned no one.

On several afternoons, when men were sitting and gossiping in the house, I watched one of them pulling at tufts of hair on the head of another man. He gathered a convenient cluster between thumb and forefinger and pulled hard on the hair. After a second or two, he moved on to another tuft, then another, until he had gone around the whole head. In this way, he was relieving the severe pain in the head of his brother-in-law. In other parts of Asmat, headaches are treated by tying rattan string tightly around the forehead. Pains in other parts of the body are ministered to with burns on the skin of the area or cuts made with the sharp edge of a clam shell.

In the jungle one day, I noticed seven leeches on my legs. The people normally brush leeches off with a twig. They see or feel their presence almost immediately, but by the time I noticed those on my ankles, they had already sunk their heads beneath the surface of my skin so that when I removed them, the blood continued to flow. One of the men searched the forest briefly and brought strawberry-like leaves and berries, rubbed both leaf and fruit over the wounds, and the blood coagulated immediately.

A wave of depression engulfed me after a week's stay. What was I doing there? The initial exhilaration of contact with Yoshigipi, the mysterious moment after the entrance of Derepen, the wonder of being with new people who almost certainly had never seen an outsider for more than a few seconds at a time, the excitement of collecting successfully, all passed. What was I getting out of my time there? Information, somewhat meager, yes; photographs, yes. But that seemed to be all.

For two whole days I barely moved from the house. I spent hours reading my paperback Trollope. In the past it had always been enough to sit and draw the people, the house, the jungle. But now I was in physical pain, my gut all knotted, and I thought back to other experiences, to the time in Peru when I had gone in search of the Amarakaire. I had left the Catholic mission, alone, on a trek through the jungle of the Madre de Dios that took four days, looking for a tribe whose men had slaughtered an entire village, except for the women and children they took back to their home place. No outboard motor then, no helicopters, nothing more than my legs to carry me and my bits of food. I was searching for the unknowable, something to fill the loneliness and despair, the pain that so often emptied me; I was searching for some Noble Savage, killer though I knew him to be; I was searching for peace and manhood, for the kind of freedom that would allow me to live my life with love and gentleness, and strength, too.

I had sought out the Amarakaire, just as I had sought these men of the Brazza who had killed the four Indonesians but who seemed amiable to me. I had come upon the Amarakaire at the edge of the Colorado River, seated on stones close up against the immense backdrop of the forest. They had known that I was there and awaited me, silent, still, fierce. My eyes took them in, absorbed them as they sat there, impassive as the stones on which their buttocks rested. I do not, cannot, rationalize my need to be with them, I was driven to that moment of complete vulnerability, to an openness whereby life and death were one, and it didn't matter which would come first.

The men had seen no Caucasian before me and the thrill of discovery was equal between us. The painted bodies, the long hair of the men, the beauty of their faces, all made me gasp. I stretched out a hand and touched cool flesh and the mass of men were suddenly around me, pinching, touching, rubbing, examining, just as I pinched, touched, rubbed, examined, laughed, cried. Was that meeting universal? Were these gestures of inspection and revelation part of all mankind? I did not think of any reaction but simply opened myself and accepted all that came my way.

I was already in my thirties at that time; still, I was no more than a child, inexperienced in the ways of the world. I had enclosed myself in a cocoon of my own making, but when I began living in the forest with my Amarakaire friends, the chrysalis that was myself began developing and I was able to shake off my protective covering, at least for the months I was there. I had found myself with people who did not understand me but accepted me as I was. I did not understand them either but I could watch the whole surface of their lives move in front of me and take part in it, too. I could eat and sleep and go hunting; I could touch and fondle and be enveloped in arms and legs and lives, and it did not matter that there was no intellectual comprehension or stimulation between us.

We went on a raid once. I did not know where we were going but suddenly after a day's walk we were attacking people, and men and women were killed. I soon realized that I was part of the group that had done this; it didn't matter that I had not, of my own accord, lifted a spear to plunge it through a living body, but instead vomited and shook with emotions I will never understand. I had reached an epiphany and had passed it by. My life had been solid; I was a rock. Suddenly, it shattered and dissolved. I left soon after that episode and my memory tends to eliminate that violence, dwelling only on the beauty of my relationship with the men. And yet I would not remove even that violent incident from my experience.

There, like in Asmat, it was not possible for me to become close to the women. It might have happened at another time when my friend Akatpitsjin asked me to sleep with his wife when we were almost true bond friends. He had, in fact, already been calling me *mbai* in front of everyone and often slept with me on my mat, coming late at night into the house in which I stayed, so as not to disturb the others there. He took me by the hand and led me to his wife and I lay with her but, oh! how quickly it became obvious that nothing could happen. Perhaps the smells that emanated from her, the shyness on her part and my own fears combined to weaken and embarrass me. Akatpitsjin stretched out next to me, leaning on an elbow, leaning onto me, his right hand on my shoulder, his left exploring my groin to test my excitement. I was flushed, my heart pounding, aware that this might be a test that I was failing, that had I been capable of intercourse with *her*, I would have been closer to *him*, that we would have been bond friends until the death of one of us.

No fires gave enough light to see a smile or frown from Akat-pitsjin; yet I knew he was not upset. Instead, we changed places and he was my proxy. I felt closer to them both then, as if I had fulfilled my role, just as in Peru, a friend had taken me by the hand to a dead man lying on the floor during that raid and, to-gether, our four hands on a single spear, we had pushed its point deep into his flesh.

In Kodna, in the midst of my deep depression, I saw an end to my life. What was I doing there? What had I been doing there all the years of my existence? Why was I not settled in New York, paint-ing, writing, loving, being loved? Why had I not stayed with that friend I had professed to love so many years ago, instead of spending six months crossing the Sahara? What other loves had I rejected in favor of searching the wilderness for whatever could ease the restless spirits within me? Is there now a friend close by with whom I can share love, who changes my life and shows me a world that has lain dormant inside me? I look back now from a still more distant viewpoint and I see the inevitable movement of all men into the world of colliding cultures, erupting environments, change and greed. I looked around then and saw Yoshigipi, his eyes smiling back into mine, a sweetness there and now trust, too. Where would he be ten years from that moment? When we met, he had already learned all he needed to know to survive in the forest; he knew the foods he could gather, the plants he could put into the ground and wait for them to grow and yield, the way to protect his life and property; perhaps he had even fought and killed. Where is he now? Wearing shorts and shirt, entering a church on Sunday? Where would his strength and fierceness be? My Amarakaire friends were gone a few years after I left them, killed by the voracious road-builders of Brazil and Peru. What would happen here when the wooding reached the Brazza, when the oil derricks were built, when the Javanese and the Makassarese came to exploit the land? The melancholy that came over me extended itself in all directions and I thought of myself as an exploiter, too. Had I not come to take away pieces of their lives, as well as their artifacts? What did I give them in return but pieces of steel and tobacco as well as opening the way for others to exploit them. I resolved nothing. Gloom surrounded me like a cocoon. I remained another day or two and then left.

Chapter

ELEVEN

BACK at the seismological camp I wrote in my journal, read mysteries, and filled myself with Western foods. All the Westerners were surprised that I had turned up alive; they were terrified of the local people. Each of them, however, asked me to collect a shield the next time I went out. It wasn't easy to turn them all down. Kolcha came in from the line, went on vacation, came back. "Man, two week's work and one in Singapore at company expense," he said, "that ain't bad. And those Singapore girls, they know how to fuck, all right!" He picked up his eleventh can of beer since supper and drank down half of it.

The three helicopter pilots, veterans of Vietnam, were Americans. The others were Australians, four who led the laborers out on the lines, several running base camp, others working the seismographic equipment, or checking and repairing the choppers. Every night after supper, ritual talk among those not playing Monopoly revolved around who had had the most girls in the shortest time, where to find the best whores, who had the biggest penis, how many orgasms each could have in a single night. The Australians drank beer, usually a whole case of twenty-four cans apiece between supper and midnight. I never understood where they kept all that liquid without having to go outside every few minutes. The pilots drank whiskey with their beer and smoked grass, pleasures that regulations demanded they stop at twelve if they were flying the next day.

Late in February 1976, after Kolcha had received his last shot of penicillin for the gonorrhea he had contracted in Singapore, we went out in the helicopter, with Brian as pilot, to Line 6 Juliet, coordinates on the company map. We passed over the Kolff and Modera Rivers and dropped down to the helipad in the crotch of the Weehuizen and Eilanden Rivers. It is unlikely that any outsiders had ever been there. A platform of logs twenty by twenty feet had been built for our campsite. An open tent covered the bedding and mosquito nets, chairs, table, shortwave radio, and the single-burner stove. Martin, the cook from Flores, had set it up before our arrival. As soon as it began to get dark he took out the Butterfly pressure lamp, filled it with kerosene, poured alcohol in the cup, put a match to it, and pumped until a brilliant white lighted up the whole area. He served steaks well done, just the way I liked them, fried potatoes, corn on the cob, beer, and lemon pie.

Line 6 Juliet was one of the lines being cut, a narrow path through the jungle, hacked out by Asmat from downstream wielding parangs, or by Indonesians imported from other parts of the island. The system was known as CRD: Cutting, Rentis, Drilling—rentis meaning "to take the shortest way." The lines were perfectly straight, continuing on for twenty-five or thirty miles. The men cut a certain distance every day and returned to camp at night. Single slender logs were put down and a simple handrail served to ease and speed up walking. When the distance became too far to walk, a new camp was built ahead and work started from there. Lines were cut parallel to one another about 300 feet apart. When several had been completed, perpendicular lines were cut to form a grid. The men in front slashed at the jungle while a group behind dug holes at prescribed distances and planted one-pound sticks of dynamite. The following day a similar group carrying seismographic equipment exploded the dynamite so that sound waves could record the density of the earth down to four thousand feet. The sheets of paper that came out of the machine were later interpreted in Jakarta.

Helipads were built on the lines for the choppers that flew daily from base camp with ice, beer, steak, fresh vegetables, eggs, bread, and mail. They brought in Indonesian workmen and their food, or took them out when the lines were finished and the men had to be moved further ahead or back to camp. Other helipads, crudely put together, had been built by people in the surrounding area, hoping to attract the helicopter that would bring steel axes and knives.

Mr. Mladek, research engineer in Jakarta for American Overseas Petroleum Limited (AMOSEAS), turned up at the Senggo camp on a routine tour of his firm's holdings throughout Indonesia on the day that word was sent via radio that some Koroway people had blocked a line by cutting down trees across it. It was AMOSEAS that employed ISSA, Indonesian Surveys, S.A., the seismological company managed in the bush by van Houten. The corporation was owned fifty percent each by Standard Oil of California and Texaco, and was in Asmat on a joint venture with other companies to defray costs. Across the line the Koroway had strung human skulls and spears and arrows, as magical devices intended to terrify the enemy that was about to cut its way through garden plots and the houses that stood beyond them. I was out on the line with Kolcha when arrows flew at us as soon as the Koroway realized the devices had not frightened the white people. They had hidden themselves behind leaves and trees and could not be seen. The arrows seemed to come from all directions. Indonesian policemen, terrified, shot their rifles indiscriminately into the forest. Mladek, having heard of my friendship with the people of Kodna, radioed ahead, asking me to try and make peace. Parangs, tobacco, steel axes, clothing, and other goods were sent out by helicopter that afternoon.

No work had been done on the line since the skulls had been strung up. The next morning, the workmen were cowering when I arrived with the gifts. None of the Koroway was to be seen or heard as I advanced alone into the gardens of banana trees and taro. *"Ndein!"* I shouted into the forest. *"Ndein!"* I shouted again, and then again, turning in all directions. *"Sini dasan! Sini dasan!"* I was using the language of the people of the Brazza and did not know whether or not the Koroway understood it. "Come out!" I shouted. "Do not be afraid!"

No one answered. Nothing answered, no bird, no animal, no leaf. It was as if the sounds I'd made had hushed all living things, as if the waves of sound had rolled on and pushed everything into the distance, as if I were a stone thrown into water sending out circles of silence that pulsed and widened and weakened with distance from the core.

I continued on along a path through the gardens. The ground was solid underfoot. Beyond, three houses stood on stilts high above the ground, each much smaller than the one on the Brazza, the poles thinner and without the central tree trunk. A ladder made of a single log with narrow notches led vertically up to a porch. I climbed barefoot, the side of my foot barely fitting into each notch. The house was empty, the fire still smoking, as if the occupants had rushed out at the sound of my voice.

The inside was divided in half by a wall of bark, a wall that I later saw separated the men from the women and children. It was too high to look over but a small opening enabled the men to see what was happening on the other side. I stood there looking around, waiting, hoping that someone would come. I was suspended between two worlds, one behind me of men waiting for me to make contact and say it was all right to destroy the houses and gardens, the other ahead, of people wanting nothing more than to be left alone to cultivate their crops, to hunt, and live in peace in the jungle.

A shield stood in a corner, powerfully protecting the house with its emanations. Stone axes and adzes were wedged into crosspieces in the walls. Masses of animal remains were stuck into the sago leaf atap of the ceiling, a work of art, a canvas of fetishistic symbols that I could not help but reach out to touch, to smell and absorb the feel of spirits flowing into me. Rows of feathers, skulls, and skeletons had been arranged immaculately, by extraordinary hands that took two dozen feathers of crown pigeons, all the same blue, all the same size, and pinned them neatly into the atap, then took a dozen skulls of flying foxes and set them next to the feathers. Below were rows of rat or bandicoot skulls, arranged according to size, next to rows of densely packed black cassowary feathers alternating with yellow parrot feathers. The brown feathers of the female cassowary were in a row by themselves. Above and below were rows of bird-of-paradise feathers of different varieties, and the feathers of wild hens and other birds. Snake skeletons, whole, and perfectly intact fish skeletons were tacked to the atap with wooden pins and, off to one side, again graded according to size, were three rows of wild boar jawbones, eleven to a row. The Koroway carved no artifacts but shields and these may have been traded for; yet here on the ceiling was an astonishing show of the work of an artist's hand.

I shook off the stupor I was falling into and left two parangs, two steel axes, and several lempeng of tobacco on the floor and returned to the line. At my request, Kolcha agreed to wait twenty-four hours to see whether the gifts would be accepted and the string of human skulls removed, but I had little hope.

That night, while cicadas buzzed and other insects shrilled, Kolcha and I went to bathe in the clear icy stream a few minutes walk away. Kolcha was a rough, attractive man, with bushy eyebrows, thick sensuous lips, and a deeply lined face. He would never talk of the past in Europe. He was charming to me and to Martin ("He's the best cook the company has!"), but he was abusive with the men. He slipped off the sarong in which he usually slept. His body was densely covered with black hair but it was easy to see the hard, well-defined muscles beneath. He kept turning to face me as he soaped his body and laughed when I shivered in the cold water. "Tell me, Tobias," he said, pronouncing my name To-bee-as, as everyone in Indonesia did, "tell me what you do for fucking when you are in the jungle for such long periods." Before I had a chance to answer, three policemen arrived, each one carrying towel and soap and a machine gun. "Fuckheads!" Kolcha called them. "They carry those fucking guns with them everywhere, even to the shithouse. They're too damned trigger-happy for me!"

We slept on cots covered with heavy blankets. I thought about the Koroway and about the naked Kolcha and fell asleep before deciding whether his question at the stream was a gesture intended to bring us closer together.

At first light we went again to the end of the line, followed by the workmen. The skulls were still in place. I went on to the house and found the gifts untouched but for spears impaled on the tobacco, a sign that people wanted no contact with us. Kolcha ordered the men to proceed with the cutting of the line and my hope disappeared that they would skirt the garden and houses.

The workmen later described a house they'd seen that was much higher than any we'd seen before. Depressed about the destruction of the other houses, I decided to look for it. The workmen pointed the way and fifteen minutes later I was looking up with astonishment at a house high on a tree trunk. Measuring with my camera, I figured the floor to be about ninety feet above the ground. A ladder of sticks went up forty feet, then divided like a *Y,* one section going to what may have been the men's entrance, the other to the women's. It was a shaky, frightening climb. The house had been abandoned and contained only a human skeleton, a beautifully decorated smoking pipe, and another stunning, rectangular exhibit of feathers and bone.

On the way back to camp, I happened to meet two youths under eighteen. Both wore rattan waist bands, nose decorations with rhinoceros horn beetle projections at the tip, and loops of cassowary quills threaded with parrot's beaks and cuscus fur for earrings. Under the loads of green bananas they carried on their backs their heads were bent so they could not see ahead. They began shaking with terror the moment they saw me. They tried to run away but my offer of knives and tobacco delayed them. The gifts, however, did not lessen their fear and they soon did run off. I did not try to follow them and made no further effort then at communication with the Koroway.

Kolcha returned happily that evening with the news that the three houses had been destroyed without interference from the people. The workmen had stolen everything inside—spears, axes, adzes, bowls, and carrying bags. He had brought me a present of the shield which I promptly returned to him.

One evening at the Brazza camp, I was at the dining table, chewing on a lamb chop, listening to Stan talk about his girlfriend in Waco. He was thin and wiry, of average height, clean-shaven,

with short sandy hair and sharp, square features. He always wore
stitched boots and had bow legs, though he claimed never to have
been on a horse. He had a good eye for throwing darts.

Brian rushed in. "Hey, man!" he said to me. "I just saw something fantastic! Fantastic! A house being built. Must be over two
hundred feet long. Lots of people around and other houses too. Do
you want to go, man? I can drop you there?"

Of course my answer was yes.

"Oh, wow, man!" Stan said. "I want to go too!"

Brian was a slightly heavier version of Stan. He walked with a
swagger and I always expected him to carry a riding crop to slap
against his boots in the manner of Douglas Fairbanks, Jr. He
looked at Stan for a second and said, "Yeah, man, that's a good
idea. We can't let him go alone, anyway. He has to have someone
to protect him."

There had never been more than superficial conversation between
Stan and myself. I didn't like the idea of his coming along, partly
because I preferred to be alone and partly because he constantly
used derogatory language about the Asmat and the Indonesians,
calling them subhuman. I was not antagonistic toward him but
simply did not like him and did not know how he might react to
people who had had no outside contact.

So it was settled without my saying anything. "You'll have to
jump from the chopper because there ain't no place to set 'er
down."

We went off two days later, after the day's work was done. We
flew up the Brazza, turned west, and crossed the Friendship River.
The mountains were immediately in front of us. We could see a
small lake with no houses around it, no canoes, no evidence of
fishing paraphernalia. To the west was a vast open space with a
long house and two smaller ones. "There it is!" yelled Brian.

People were running along the logs, scattering in all directions.
Men seemed to be rushing into the long house, women into the
jungle to hide with the children. The wings of the chopper
churned up the attap roofs and I feared they would blow away.

The doors of the helicopter had been removed and left at the
camp to facilitate jumping out. Below us, the clearing was a

jumbled mass of huge treetrunks and stumps, branches and vegetation. There was no way to land. When we were down to about fifteen feet, I threw out the bundle of parangs, axes, tobacco, and other goods with which I hoped to trade. I worried for a moment about the Uher tape recorder, too heavy to throw out and too bulky to jump with since I was already burdened with still camera and Super 8. I left it in the chopper.

I jumped out first, naked except for sneakers. Stan jumped wearing jeans and boots. The helicopter climbed to about a hundred and fifty feet. The plan was for me and Stan to jump out; Brian would hover above us until we saw whether the people were friendly or not. If they were hostile, the chopper would come right down and we would climb up a rope into it.

We waited for some of the men to come out of the forest or from the houses, but nothing happened. The only noise or movement was from the chopper and from us. It was obvious that nothing would happen while the helicopter was there. I signaled Brian and he flew off, leaving us alone.

It was not long before the first men came warily out of the long house. At first they stood and watched us. I took up one of the parangs and held it out. The men began walking back and forth. They ran short distances, shot arrows into the air, jumped up and down. They tossed clouds of white lime into the air from reed tubes. They screamed and shouted, whooped and yelled. The atmosphere was suddenly galvanic and exhilarating.

The men ran toward us, then ran back. I waved the parang, offering it to whoever would come and take it. I shouted, *"Ndein! Ndein!"* They came closer, ran back, pointed their bows and arrows and spears at us, shot the arrows and threw the spears above our heads. The hullabaloo was deafening. I shouted again, *"Ndein! Ndein!* Come! Come on!"

The excitement became frenzied. I yelled as loudly as did the men; I was exalted and ebullient as each time they came toward us they came closer. Soon I could see the sticks studded with coix seeds jutting from their nostrils.

Suddenly one of the men rushed up, took the parang from my

hand, and ran back to the others as if afraid that I would demand its return. I smiled and laughed and jumped up and down. They came up to us screaming, whooping in unison, "Whuh! Whuh! Whuh!" It was a sound so vast and impassioned it drowned out the world. The men were so close around us that the sound surrounded us, reverberated against the walls of the forest, and bounced back to increase the din. We stared at one another, we touched and slapped one another.

The great noise, the magnificent chorale, died down and the men were almost speaking and laughing in normal tones. I heard then the squeaky voice on my right, "Tobias! Tobias! Let's get the fuck out of here! They're going to kill us!" Seconds later the same voice said, "Damn! I've just shit in my pants!"

In the evening, in the immense, unfinished men's house, we sat on pandanus mats, Stan and I, both of us naked. Stan had washed himself and his jeans and felt at ease. We were close to the central fireplace where the men brought us sago and pig meat. I traded for a shield and two drums, always handing out tobacco with the other goods and leaving some on the floor for everyone to smoke. The men talked throughout the night, one of them singing of the day's events and probably telling stories of past glories in war. Stan insisted that he had never been so frightened in his life, not even during the war in Vietnam, and he could not understand why I had not been terrified too. "They were shooting their fucking arrows at us, weren't they?"

It had been an exceptionally raucous Asmat greeting, for the people were indeed Asmat. The welcome may have been violent but not so different from the welcomes with which the people downstream used to greet visitors, this same kind of warlike display, arrows shot in ceremonial fashion the prescribed number of times. "Sure," I said, "you're right. They were scared by the helicopter, of course. But once it was gone, we were alone without weapons. They knew the advantage was theirs, even though they did not know what magic we might perform.

"Admittedly, they were cautious about coming up for the first parang, but once they'd accepted it their fear was gone and they began to take real pleasure in our arrival and the things we brought. Sure, they might have killed us at any time but they had no reason to, and they were certainly curious about us, and what we had with us." Stan's contribution to the trade goods had been several rolls of the yellow cap wire which fascinated all the men.

Later he picked up one of his boots and sheepishly took out a small revolver. "Shit, man. I had this ready. I had it in the side of my boot all the time, ready to use. And I would have used it except that I was so scared I forgot about it until I took off the fucking boots!"

Lying on a mat that night, trying to sleep, but instead going over the day's events in my mind, I thought of our different reactions to the same scene, how I had accepted the incredible uproar as a grand ritual reception, while Stan, with no experience of the area and a head full of headhunting and cannibal tales, could only cringe in fear of being decapitated. I tried to visualize Captain Cook's arrival in Asmat, perhaps welcomed in this same fashion. Perhaps his men in the two longboats had misinterpreted the painted faces, the noise, the bows and arrows and spears just as Stan had done.

We dozed and woke every few minutes to the sound of drumming, singing, talking. Brian returned in the helicopter two days later and the men disappeared again. Brian let down a knotted rope and we climbed up.

At the camp, Stan delighted everyone every day during the next couple of months with the tale of our expedition. He described in detail his own fear being so intense that he had emptied his bowels into his pants. He was proud of having done so; it was proof of the fearsome predicament in which he'd found himself.

AMOSEAS, assured by the seismographic experts that oil was to be found at the confluence of the Kolff and Eilanden Rivers, built an air-conditioned city in this area where the people had rarely seen outsiders and were still living traditional lives. Floodlights burned and drilling machines worked throughout the day and night. The drills bore down to five thousand feet and found only water. Half a year later, the city was dismantled and every sign of its existence disappeared.

Chapter

TWELVE

UPSTREAM on the Brazza and the
other rivers that fed into the upper Siretsj, my mood changed constantly. Collecting artifacts became an obsession and I was greedy,
not wanting anyone from the outside to share in the experience of
searching out shields and information on symbols. The bishop, Al,
sometimes went with me, a somewhat different persona in his red
shorts and pith helmet from the man in mitre and alb. He collected his own information on the cultures we visited and made
word lists everywhere. His wit was always sharp and spontaneous,
often directed at me. In Ketta, the Awyu, men with enormous,
elongated noses stretched like the lower lips of Ubangi women and
accomodating three plugs of bamboo, provoked him into saying,
in his matter-of-fact way, "Well, well. Finally, here is someone
with a nose larger than Tobias's."

The artifacts I collected were often divided into three groups:
one for the museum in Agats, one for the Crosier Asmat Museum
in Hastings, Nebraska, and one for a German couple, Ursula and
Gunter Konrad, friends of the bishop who became friends of mine
as well. They had been in Asmat several times and were among the
first to explore the Brazza River. They had a keen scientific interest
in the people, though their first trip had been to collect birds and
animals for the University of Heidelberg. Over the years, they also
collected shields and artifacts that are now in Heidelberg in a museum built for them. They were always generous: had donated an
X-ray machine to the hospital, gave me a Leicaflex when a canoe in
which I was traveling sank with my camera, sent Christmas gifts
to all the missionaries every year, and gave shields and other important items, including a collection of stuffed animals—a cuscus,

cockatoos, hornbills—to the museum in Agats. Everyone who passed through Germany was always welcome to spend days at the Konrads' home, being entertained lavishly and taken on tours of Heidelberg and the surrounding countryside.

Although I was greedy about collecting and for a while felt everything was my own, I soon came to understand that my great pleasure was not in possession but rather in amassing fifty or sixty shields and other artifacts on each trip. Once the carvings were back in Agats, it was not of prime importance that many of them left Asmat, as long as they were not used for financial gain. I did on rare occasions hope that certain pieces would go to Hastings rather than to Heidelberg, but such are the mysteries of friendship. By then, the museum in Agats had representative examples of almost everything in Asmat and the storeroom was full; I accepted only carvings that were needed to round out the collection.

While I worked in Agats cataloguing, a disturbing tension sometimes existed between Bram, the curator, and myself, which depressed me enough to try to change whatever I was doing that appeared wrong in his eyes. It may be that I was overbearing without realizing it or that I was not humble enough in my role as researcher/cataloguer. Bram never confronted me with this directly but went his own way, taking no interest in the artifacts and spending his time with the people. He was not only curator of the museum, but also lay pastor of the village of Sjuru, where he lived in a fine house, a fifteen-minute walk from the museum in good weather. He spent more time with his parishioners than with his curatorial responsibilities; often the carvings in the storeroom were so infested with silverfish, roaches, and other insects, that they disintegrated in my hands, like the Trojan warrior who turned to dust when exposed to air. Bram had been a theological student in Merauke when the bishop began his search for a curator. The Archbishop of Merauke suggested Bram, who immediately agreed to go for training in Honolulu and New York after he received his B.A. in Theology. Since Bram was a Muyu from the mountains, and since mountain people of New Guinea usually have no carvings of any kind other than bows, arrows, and spears, it is not surprising that he had no understanding of or interest in the art of Asmat. This became a problem in his relationship with the museum, for his position as pastor always took precedence over museum work— perhaps rightly so—and he kept his office there open to parishioners throughout the day. It was invariably full of visitors from Sjuru.

A meeting between Bram, Eric Sarkol, the assistant curator, Trenk, advisor to the museum, and myself, after my first year's stay, brought out Bram's resentment toward me, his feeling that I had usurped his position and had taken over the running of the museum. Trenk pointed out that from the beginning, long before my arrival, Bram had shown no interest in the carvings or in display or conservation or in any of the aspects of the curatorship for which he had been trained. Trenk felt, too, that I had kept myself in the background during my first months in order to give Bram time to feel his way into the job without pressure from any outsider, that I had worked on displays with Eric at his, Trenk's, direction only after Bram had not responded to our attempts at getting him involved.

Bram was also discontent because of the church's stand against his becoming a priest after his marriage. He had been advised early on in his novitiate that Catholic priests were necessarily celibate. He had been warned again after he began working at the museum, after he met someone he decided to marry, that if he did so he could never be ordained a priest. Nevertheless, after his marriage, he resented the Crosiers as if it were their order that had set up the prohibition, rather than the papacy itself.

I never failed to go to the museum even when periods of depression came over me. I calmed myself by drawing artifacts and by recognizing symbols and villages from which they came. There was an enormous satisfaction in leaning a shield against the shelving so that it caught the light in a way that defined the reliefs on its surface. I measured its height and width carefully, scaled these down to fit onto the 5″ × 8″ catalogue card on which I worked, quickly sketched the outline and designs, and proceeded to draw in pen and ink.

Sometimes, at night, I walked to the bishop's house for a beer and an enlivening conversation or listened to his jokes, well told. We discussed Bram often, both of us saddened by his inability to understand the need to conserve the artifacts for future generations of Asmat. When I was not at the museum, Bram confided in Eric; Eric later brought these confidences to me. Most often they had something to do with my catalogue system or with the certainty that I was a spy for the CIA, a rumor Bram apparently started and talked over with the camat. I worried for a while what the government would do if they believed the story, but the reports that I was to be thrown out of the country came to nothing.

The bishop, too, had periods of depression. They might concern problems between the Indonesians and the Asmat or between himself and one or more of his Crosiers. He talked to me frankly about the men and asked my opinion about whatever disputes or personal difficulties might come up. He was—in my presence, at any rate—the most open-minded of the missionaries there and did not complain bitterly as others did when *papisj* was discovered taking place in a village. He recognized the fact that a people could not change their whole way of thinking within a few years. I opened up to him, too, about most of the information I was gathering. He was not in the least prudish and wanted me to write a paper on the material I had collected on Asmat sexual life. When I said that some Fathers would not only have trouble assimilating the information but would try to stop certain practices if they found out what was going on, he suggested writing for an anthropological journal so obscure that it might never be seen or heard of in Asmat.

I liked the bishop and liked to travel with him. It also gave me great pleasure to call him by his first name, Al. He never lost his sense of humor when upstream and used his time wisely in accumulating knowledge. We sometimes had heated discussions on language or variations in the cultural life. During one of our trips together with Father Ed Greiwe and Father Virgil Petermeier, we spent a night in a village where a *basu suangkus* feast was going on, the beginnings of which I had seen weeks earlier. I insisted on my

Bishop Alphonse Sowada in full regalia for Mass.

Father Trenkenschuh in center, with the bishop at left, in Ajam.

Woman rinsing and squeezing sago from the pulp of the
sago tree.

Cutting out a small window in a felled sago tree into which
the owner will put moss that has been rubbed over his anus
and armpits.

Women with bamboo tubes of drinking water from the swamp.

Gossiping on the porch in the late afternoon.

Women fishing with nets in the Ewta River.

Adoption ceremony at the moment when the adopted individual crawls over the backs of the new fathers and through the legs of the mothers that form the birth canal.

Akatpitsjin, my informer and friend.

One of my adopted brothers in Japtambor.

Bride being carried into the house of the groom by the mother's brother. Note the bride price stone axe on her shoulder and the three pairs of boar's tusks at her uncle's elbow that indicate he has taken three heads in battle.

Bringing mangrove trees to the village at the beginning of an ancestor pole feast.

Uppermost figure on an ancestor pole from Buepis.

Ancestor poles in the village of Bajun.

Detail of a face on an ancestor pole.

A fight had begun between two villages.

Drawing of body mask from Iroko.

Young man painted in traditional fashion for initiation in Ajam.

Shield being brought down from house in Amarou.

First known photograph of women on the Brazza River, 1976.

Climbing a notched log ladder in Amarou.

Interior of house in Tajan.

Lamalo smoking his pipe in Tajan.

Two men in Tajan.

Awju man with three bamboo nose plugs.

spelling and pronunciation of the word *"suangkus,"* while he insisted that there was no such combination of consonants in Asmat as "ngk." The carvings made for this feast were logs with heads carved at both ends; the words *basu suangkus* I had translated as "the making visible of the heads of men who have been killed in battle." After listening to more than a dozen men pronounce that middle *"g,"* the bishop had to admit defeat. However, he got back at me later over the pronunciation of Yoshigipi's name after meeting him on the Brazza River. "No!" he insisted. "His name is Yosigipi. You aren't listening properly. For heaven's sake, his two front teeth are missing and he's lisping!" Somewhat shamefaced, I had to give in.

Although I thought the mission remarkable in building a museum in Agats for the Asmat themselves, with little thought for tourists, since there were only a handful the year it opened, I could not always agree with its policies, just as the missionaries themselves must have had reservations about my own behavior—what they thought I might be doing, rather than what they knew.

In Tiau, on the Dairam River, we once stopped to pay our respects to the Dutch minister. He and the bishop had a prolonged discussion on the areas of Protestant and Catholic control, and who was to have dominion over certain peoples and certain rivers. I must have been distracted during the conversation for I thought they were saying, "I'll give you the Brazza people, if you'll give me the Kombai between the Dairam Hitam and the Dairam Kabur." It sounded like an agreement at Yalta. It also sounded like the story one of the missionaries brought back from Jakarta of eight generals dividing Irian Jaya into eight equal parts, each general to exploit his own part in his own way.

Sometimes I irritated everyone with my enthusiasm.

It was my habit to rise early in the mappi, while it was still dark and the others still asleep. I could perform my ablutions at the stern without having to rush, without any embarrassment about noises I might make. I shaved as soon as it got light.

I was squatting comfortably in the blackness of night, balanced on the soles of my feet, my buttocks hanging over the water, when

I saw the forest on my left blinking with fireflies—hundreds, thousands of them, all blinking on and off at the same time. It was a breathtaking moment. I had seen this spectacle once before and had later reported it to an entymologist who had been searching for years without luck for this kind of synchronous firefly display. I tried calling out but in my excitement my voice caught in my throat several times before I was able to use it properly. "Everybody up! Everybody up! Those fireflies are here! The ones I saw in Atsj! They're here! Get up, you lazy bums! It's fantastic!"

"Oh, shut up, for Christ's sake!" came the first answer.

"Leave us alone!" came the next.

"Go back to sleep and stop bothering us!"

"*Ngetot!*" (Fuck!)

Dawn crept up while I crouched there and the lights of the fireflies faded and went out. I hooked up my mirror to a nail and began to shave.

Chapter

THIRTEEN

IN 1978, Jorgen Heuter wrote to me from Europe, asking whether I would be interested in guiding him and a friend into the unexplored territory of the upper Brazza. Jorgen, a great hulk of a man about forty years old, with a huge belly that did not seem to impede his movements, had been a friend in years past. We had met atop a pyramid at Uxmal during a trip he was making from one Mayan ruin to another, while I was seeing the sights of Yucatán before starting on a walk across the peninsula from Campeche to Bacalar and Chetumal.

In his letter to me, Jorgen offered to pay all expenses but could not afford a salary. The bishop thought it a good opportunity to collect for the museum, so I wrote back agreeing to the plan and made arrangements with Manu Lamera for canoes, outboard motors, and all the necessary food and gear. Two months later Jorgen arrived with his friend Bruno Teller. They looked to be the antithesis of one another—Jorgen big, blond, and always smiling, with a way of blinking his eyes that seemed to mean good humor; Bruno short, dark, of splendid physique, brooding, often silent for long periods.

We set off in two canoes, both with Yamaha motors, Jorgen, Bruno, Manu, and myself in one with food and fresh water, the other loaded with fuel drums, cartons of food, and camping equipment, and manned by two of Manu's many bright relatives, Nor and Paskalis. For two days we traveled, for the most part, in a heavy rain, stopping briefly at two villages that were empty, the people out cutting wood for Fajar Harapan, one of the logging companies. In Wooi Nor and Paskalis banked their canoe, and stayed there with most of the food and fuel while the rest of us took on the goods necessary for ten days and went on to spend the night in Senggo, where we put up our tarpaulin tent on one of the rafts that would be floated down to the mouth of the Siretsj when a logging ship appeared. We went to the government office for permission to travel upstream, then proceeded up the Dairam River to Tiau, arriving in the early afternoon.

Mrs. Schoeldhof, wife of the Dutch minister with whom the bishop had made the deal dividing up the river people, was standing at the bank of the river in her faded print dress, stockings, and shoes. She greeted us with a nod and said her husband was too busy to see us. "He is working on his sermon for Sunday and cannot be wasting time with visitors." She had deep crevices of bitterness on her face.

Jorgen got out of the canoe, marched up to her, and said, "We don't ask anything of you. We don't need you."

Mr. Schoeldhof suddenly appeared behind her and insisted that we come immediately to the house for tea. His wife shouted something in Dutch, but he motioned for us to follow him. In spite of her antagonism, she made tea and offered delicious-looking cookies that we left untouched. Schoeldhof himself was pleasant and informative about the area in which we wanted to travel, and both were interested in my notebook when I showed them drawings of shield designs, and word lists.

"All that land between the Dairam Hitam and the Dairam Kabur," said Mr. Schoeldhof in his strong Dutch accent, "is called Tajan and has a thousand people living in tree houses. We have been able to make contact with only a few. We go in the helicopter and leave axes and parangs, nylon and fishhooks. The people take them to the river and tie them up with bows and arrows and that means, 'Stay away! We don't want you here!' But we will go back one day soon and try again."

Bruno impolitely asked for a place to sleep that night but there was no invitation forthcoming.

While we were getting into the canoe, a young Indonesian came up and greeted Manu by name, as if they were old friends. He was about twenty, small and compact, with a hard, active body. His curly hair burst out around his face and his large front teeth seemed just right between his thick lips.

Manu introduced him. "This is Idris, better known as Nyong. He does wooding for Fajar Harapan up here. He wants to come along. Says he speaks Kombai."

My reaction was instantaneous and I said, "No!" Jorgen's response was just as quick: "Oh, yes! We need someone who speaks the language."

Bruno said nothing at first, then asked me, "Why don't you want him along?"

"We don't want anyone with us who is into wooding. I do not want to be responsible for exploiting the people of the Brazza or anywhere else we might go."

Jorgen, who had been to Indonesia before and spoke some of the language, questioned Nyong, who promised to say nothing to the people about cutting logs. He wanted to come along to help, without payment.

"Look, Jorgen," I put in. "I don't believe him. Maybe I'm wrong, but we will be visiting friends of mine. Even if he doesn't mention wooding on this trip, he will have been under my auspices and the people will trust him. If he is wooding here for Fajar Harapan, he will be doing the same thing upstream. So far, the Indonesians have been too frightened to go up there. It would be immoral and unethical to take him along."

Jorgen preferred to believe Nyong, hoping that through him we would have easier contact with the people.

The vote Jorgen, Bruno and I took went against me and Nyong left us for his belongings. He returned a few minutes later wearing a red batik shirt, flared trousers, and shoes. A rolled umbrella, wrapped in plastic, was sticking out of the bundle made of his sleeping mat.

No sooner had we started on our way than Jorgen became irritated with Bruno. "What did you mean by saying that we'd like to spend the night? We don't want anything to do with missionaries." He and Bruno addressed unkind remarks to each other all evening.

In the morning the argument continued but changed direction.
"You gave the teacher too much money for one night!" Bruno insisted about the payment for sleeping at a teacher's house.

"Cheapskate!" countered Jorgen.

We were on the Dairam Kabur, the White Dairam. We passed
deserted houses high in trees, then houses with smoke seeping
through their roofs.

"Let's stop here," said Bruno.

"No," said Jorgen. "Let's go on."

"*Sheis!*" said Bruno.

"Damnit, Bruno! Nyong says the people farther up are more
interesting."

The arguments always stopped when we were with people of the
area. They excited all of us and our cameras kept us too busy to
think about one another. We stopped in Sagis, a small village with
four or five small houses at the river's edge. Eleven men were on
the bank waiting for us.

We quickly unloaded our patrol boxes and trade goods, and took
them into the vacant teacher's house. The men watched us and
helped carry the parangs and axes, commenting on the sharpness of
their blades. When we finished unloading, the men suddenly
grouped themselves into a phalanx and began walking along the
sandy beach. They continued on about a hundred feet, turned,
walked back faster, grunting at the same time, "Whuh! Whuh!
Whuh!" The man in front carried a shield high above his head. At
the end of the stretch of beach they turned again, ran back, and
yodeled a plaintive tune of four notes. The yodel changed back to
"Whuh! Whuh!" and two groups were exclaiming it rapidly in
two different tones, one after the other. They jumped into the air
with their knees bent stiffly, their hands on knees and thighs.
They broke up into small groups that crisscrossed in zigzag patterns. They ran, jumped, grunted, yodeled.

Back at the teacher's house, the arguments began again while we
were putting up our mosquito nets and preparing supper. Manu
got angry with Nyong for taking too long to wash the rice. Jorgen
got mad at Manu for giving orders to Nyong. Bruno said that

Manu was in charge of cooking and gear and had every right to tell Nyong what to do. The men of Sagis came in with sago and shrimp, which we exchanged for rice and hot sardines in tomato sauce. They told us that the Kombai lived in the jungle not far away and we arranged for guides to take us there.

The following morning the men danced and chanted on the beach while we climbed into our canoe. Not more than ten minutes upstream, we banked the dugout and entered the blackness of the swamp.

For the first half of the two-and-a-half-hour walk, we trudged through water to our knees, with thorns and prickles everywhere. Then without warning everything changed, and we were walking easily on dry land, within great stands of red sago palms, different from the thorned variety downstream, with tree trunks that reached fifteen or more feet above the ground before spreading their leaves. We were in the land of the Kombai.

Four houses made up the Kombai hamlet of Amarou. They stood at the four corners of an immense clearing, with the structures at unequal distances from one another. They were on stilts and tree trunks, more than forty feet high, the houses reached by a single vertical notched log. A man stood behind the log ladder, as if hiding. He ran into the forest, called out and received a yodel in reply. There was silence then. Nothing moved, nothing called or flew or ran through the jungle. We stood perfectly still, only our eyes moving, trying to penetrate the dense growth, watching for someone to return. Dried leaves crackled and a man appeared, staring at us from behind leaves. He looked cross-eyed and had three long tresses of hair hanging down to the sides of his nose. Human or animal teeth were tied to the ends of the tresses. The rest of his hair was interwoven with strands of sago leaf and was cut in a short bob with fringes covering his forehead. From the sides of his nostrils long wooden stems like straws protruded at forty-five degree angles. Five or six loops of cassowary quills hung from his earlobes. He stared with a force that might have opened a pathway through the vegetation. Even from thirty feet away we could see his lips quivering. We called to him and he shouted back, "Yuh!"

I held out tobacco and a parang and he yelled again. I moved closer and he came out into the clear space. He took the machete, examined it carefully, ran his tongue along the blade, smelled it, then climbed up to the house.

I hesitated at first to make the climb but I had learned when traveling from the Brazza camp that by putting an inch or two of the side of my foot into the notch, it was not difficult.

The inhabitants of the hamlet, terrified, had run into the jungle and had been watching our movements from hidden places. None of the women or children came back but six men returned, two of them carrying shields with designs like those on the shields of the Tjitak. They were, in fact, so similar that I wondered whether they *had* been made by Tjitak carvers and traded to the Kombai.

I exchanged the usual goods for the shields and learned that the spiral designs represented swirling water, as they did among the Tjitak. We spent most of the day gathering information, then returned to Sagis.

Four men of Emembi were there for the night. They were on their way to Djawok to cut wood for Bahar of the Fajar Harapan Company. As soon as they mentioned Bahar, Nyong laughed and lamented their loss of time and energy.

"Bahar will never pay you. You are wasting your time." He was interrupted by shouting and yelping that came from Jorgen and Bruno who were bathing with two men who had accompanied us from Amarou. "You must cut wood for me," Nyong was saying. "You ask the people of Senggo. Ask the people of Tiau and Mbinerbis. You will not be paid. You will work hard and will get only a pair of shorts and some tobacco. You should sell the wood to me."

One of the men of Emembi brought a twenty-five-rupiah coin and asked for a shirt in exchange. The coin was worth about two U.S. cents.

"You see! You see!" shouted Nyong. "That's not worth anything. They are cheating you. You should cut wood only for me!"

After his bath in the river, Jorgen listened to the discussion and said to me, "Now, how can you complain when he is trying to help teach the people the value of money? As long as they are already cutting wood, wouldn't it be better for them to cut for Nyong? At least he won't cheat them."

It was pointless to argue. We awoke the next morning without the usual clatter around us. No one came to cadge food or watch us shave or cook. Manu soon discovered that eight parangs were missing and that all the people had disappeared into the jungle. Everyone blamed everyone else for not guarding the goods properly during the night.

Even in the midst of these disagreeable circumstances, the collecting was going well. We already had eleven shields. It had been arranged among us that the artifacts would be divided up into four groups. Assuming that all continued in this same way, Jorgen, Bruno and I would each take six shields; whatever was left over would go to the museum in Agats.

I had with me the hundred-word Kombai list the bishop had made on our own trips into the area; it was indispensable for gathering information. I added to the list but Nyong had exaggerated his knowledge of the language and contributed nothing.

It was in Tajan that I thought the wrangling between Jorgen and Bruno would finally explode. Nyong had become Jorgen's personal attendant the moment he joined us. He quickly ingratiated himself with Jorgen and ignored the rest of us. He blew up Jorgen's air mattress with the foot pump, put up his mosquito net, washed his dishes, arranged his belongings and, in general, made his life much easier. I usually put out the Butterfly lamp and was the last to crawl into my mosquito net at night.

Nothing could convince Jorgen that Nyong was talking to the men in the middle of the night. Almost nightly, I woke to hear Nyong telling the men that they would have axes and parangs, tobacco and clothing by cutting down a few trees for him. Jorgen never noticed that Nyong crawled out of his net and later crawled back in again. Neither he nor Bruno was ever disturbed by noise or movement once they were asleep.

One night we slept in the house of Lamalo and his family in Tajan. Lamalo and his two wives and one child watched with astonishment as the air mattress expanded with air, were amazed at the mosquito nets, and were delighted to taste and share our food. Everyone fell asleep immediately on the sheets of sago spathe that were their beds. I too fell asleep within seconds but soon heard the floor creaking and then the sound of footsteps. Kombai houses appear flimsy; they sway in the wind and shake with any movement. Even so they are strong. Still, I wake up easily.

Later, before dawn, I awoke to the soft sound of voices. With a little concentration, I could make out the voice of Nyong trying to explain wooding to Lamalo who, fortunately, understood nothing that was said. I was tempted to shout out and wake Jorgen up to prove that Nyong had his discussions with the people about wood, but Nyong would surely claim he'd gotten up to relieve his bladder.

Weeks passed and the problems continued. We went up the Brazza and the Kolff, up the Modera and the Steenboom. We sometimes walked a whole day to reach new people.

I deeply resented Nyong. He was making friends everywhere. We finally left him in Wooi and returned to Agats. Jorgen gave him an air mattress, a radio, and some canned goods, but Nyong asked for money, demanding a daily wage for his work. Bruno fumed and said that he had joined us claiming he wanted no money. It did not surprise me that he got his way.

Back in Agats, as soon as Jorgen and Bruno left, Manu scandalized the town with tales of the arguments we all had. Months later we heard that the people of the Brazza were cutting wood for Nyong. The bishop pointed an accusing finger at me. "You're responsible!" he exclaimed. I was horrified, even though I had expected it to happen. Then news reached us that Nyong had been killed by the people working for him. Justice, I thought. Nyong's sister had heard that I had taken photographs of him and sent a message asking for a copy of one.

Chapter

FOURTEEN

"DAMNIT, you guys!" said the young and handsome Father Dan Davidson. "Don't you realize how anti-Indonesian you are? Don't you realize how you bad-mouth them all the time? Don't you think it possible for there to be one good Indonesian, one who is not as rotten as you say they all are?"

Father Davidson had come from the Crosier House in Minneapolis to lead a retreat. He had been in Agats a week when he announced a meeting to discuss the personal attitudes and lives of the Fathers and Brothers. I had not expected to attend any of the sessions since I was neither Catholic nor a member of any order. Yet I had been asked to sit in on this one. The question of animosity toward the Indonesians was a touchy one and sometimes caused disagreements among the Crosiers, some of whom believed that justice would best be served by speaking out against corruption and wrongful acts, that indeed it was an act of omission and therefore sinful not to do so, while others feared they would be thrown out of the country if they failed to maintain friendly relations with all government officials at all times. Each of the Crosiers was aware of his own prejudices, but no one said anything in defense of himself. Instead the men lowered their eyes and shifted in their chairs. The few smokers lit their cigarettes and coughed. After a long silence, Father Davidson suggested that the men examine their consciences in an effort to overcome their unchristian feelings. They might also think about spending more time, he said, with Indonesians who might have something positive to offer. All of us had separated the Indonesians from the Asmat, though of course the Asmat were Indonesians, too.

Later, at midday dinner, I sat next to Father Davidson. "Dan," I said, "excuse me for putting my two cents in, but everyone feels the same way about the Indonesians and I am no better than the rest of them. Much as I hate to admit it, I am also prejudiced. However, I do have an explanation for myself; not an excuse, mind you, only an explanation."

"Go on," he prompted when I paused.

"You've been here only a few days and haven't seen the beatings or heard the stories of the camat who shot off the earlobes of those who would not cut wood for him, so be patient with those who do have firsthand knowledge. I didn't want to say anything in front of the others since I'm not really part of the group. Even so, my own experiences may be relevant."

We finished our vegetable soup and got up to serve ourselves from bowls of pig meat, string beans, and rice. For dessert there were pumpkin pies. When we sat down again, I went on. "I've been coming to Indonesia for years and I love the place. The first time was for a stunning six months. I arrived in Sumatra by ferry from Penang in Malaya. I took the bus to Lake Toba, went to Sibolga on the west coast, sailed on a tiny boat to the island of Nias for a month, and returned to Sibolga on the same boat, sleeping on foul-smelling sheets of crude rubber. I loved it. Then I went down to Padang by bus and finally by ship past Krakatao on the way to Jakarta. Marvelous! Another time I went slowly through Java and later spent six weeks in Bali and, on my third trip I think it was, went to Celebes, lived with the Toradja above Rantapao, went east to the island of Halmahera, and down to Bandaneira, original capital of the Spice Islands, with its cloves, nutmeg, and mace. Every moment was wonderful. There were beautiful Indonesians everywhere, people I could never have anything against. Not only could I say nothing against them, I could only give them praise. They took me in everywhere; they were gentle and hospitable and generous and all the good things one likes to think about people.

"Now, suddenly, I am in the position of looking at myself and saying that I am anti-Indonesian.

"Sitting in the rec room, I listened to you berate us for being anti-Indonesian and I thought of my own prejudices against the Germans because so many of my family had been killed during World War II. I had always thought I had good reasons for that prejudice until a friend of mine invited me to visit him in Cologne when he heard that I was going to Czechoslovakia to see an aunt-by-marriage. Her husband, my father's brother, had died in a furnace during the war and his widow later wrote occasional letters to my father. Once a year, at her request, he sent several plum-colored skeins of wool which she knitted into warm pullovers for her family. After my father's death, I found her address among his papers and wrote to her. She suggested my stopping in Trebic if I ever got to Europe. I decided to go.

"It was then that my friend asked me to stay with him for a few days in Cologne. The idea horrified me. Go to *Germany?* I said to myself. Where the *Germans* live? Impossible! Too many of the family were gone; too many had been killed in concentration camps. But, damn! I thought. Here I complain about other people's prejudices, about the rednecks and their hatred of the blacks, I complain about anti-Semitism, anti-Catholicism, and God knows what else, and here I am reacting the same way. So I went to Cologne and had good times with my friend, and Germany wasn't as bad as I'd feared, though my stomach was in constant turmoil during my visit. The second time I went was easier.

"And now here is another prejudice, this time against the Indonesians. I hate myself for it. You're right, of course, we *are* prejudiced and I have to stop and ask myself, Why? It was easy enough to explain about the Germans to myself, but why here? Why do I find the Indonesians here evil and abusive and infuriating? I think I have the answer for myself.

"In all my travels in this country, in all those places where I found beauty, I was with the people of the land, the people who plant the rice, who work the fields, who live with the water buffalo and the ducks, the people who make up most of the population of this country. I had no dealings with officials or the army once I'd passed through Immigration at the airport—and officials can be corrupt everywhere.

"Here in Asmat, there is a completely different race, a nation that seems to have nothing to do with the Indonesians I'd met elsewhere. No one of the land has come here. No outsiders till the soil—there *is* no soil, all of Asmat is swamp. Most of those who are here were sent by the government—the police, the army, the officials, none of whom wanted to come in the first place. For them, there is nothing here, no movies, no electricity, no night-clubs, no prostitutes, no television, not even the kind of food they are used to, except for the subsidized rice brought in. There is nothing but swamp.

"But most important, unfortunately, are the merchants and traders who have come to make money. They don't care how they go about it or how they exploit the people. No one questions the right or wrong of it. Not even the Asmat, who accept it as they would have accepted subjugation by any group in the days of head-hunting. The Indonesians are colonialists of the worst sort, as bad as any Americans with the Indians and blacks, as bad as the Australians with the aborigines, or the Germans in South Africa. There are plenty of examples around the world throughout history. Indonesians will tell you that the Asmat are animals and therefore there is nothing wrong in taking advantage of them. That's the way it is.

"All this has happened in so many places in the world you'd think that someone might have learned something. You'd think that because Indonesia itself had been a colony under the Dutch the people would have sympathy and understanding for others in the same circumstances. But it doesn't work that way. *They* are in power now, *they* are the colonialists and they are taking advantage of everyone and everything they can."

Father Davidson took in all this while nodding his head in understanding. Rightly so, however, he continued to press the men into searching out the better side of the Indonesians. He learned a great deal in his weeks of traveling around and he read copies of letters the bishop had written to the central government documenting corruption and violence against the people. I, too, wrote reports on my own travels that the bishop used when relevant.

It was Father John Fleischhacker who first got me to write reports, claiming that he himself had no time to do them. We often traveled together through his parish and I made entries in my journal every day, trying to keep up with events and information on carvings.

John was not always an easy man to be with but he was exuberant, intelligent, and very quick in his responses, not always wise ones. I liked him and we became friends. Like the bishop, he came from Minnesota and had already been in Asmat eleven years when I first met him in 1973. His parish was in the northwest, his home in Jamasj, the large village in which the Dutch lumber company had been based for close to ten years. The men of most of his parish had been cutting wood since the mid-1950s but no one had yet been taught to measure logs for payment and only a few could read and write or count money.

The first trip about which I gave the bishop a written report took place in January 1979. News had spread downstream that the people of four of John's villages had returned home after fourteen months in the jungle, to which they had fled to escape the wooding forced upon them by officials and merchants. In John's mappi, we went up to Ao on the Tsjetsj River, two days from Agats.

The village had been battered by heavy rains and strong winds during the months it had been empty, and the jungle, with no one to keep it in check, had grown in from all sides to attack everything within reach. Vines pulled at beams, creepers covered walls, trees and shrubs and fungi intruded, enveloped, wrapped, and overwhelmed everything with green and gray and brown masses of leaf and thorn and bark.

The houses all leaned in one direction, as if pushed by some great forest spirit avenging the death and destruction of its ancient ironwood trees. The attap roofs and bark floors had been blown and tossed, agitated by whirlwinds; the walls of the church, witnesses and victims of natural and demonic violence, had collapsed and dissolved into debris, and the small, lush garden of banana trees had turned dismal, its leaves torn and shredded, the trees themselves bent and rotting with overripe and dead fruit.

No one was in sight.

"Bastards!" muttered John, more to himself than to me, when it seemed that the village was deserted. "We should have known better than to come all this way without proof that the people had returned."

However the four-day trip was not completely wasted, for Urbanus Umu appeared suddenly with two other men of his family.

"Urbanus! Urbanus Umu!" John called when he saw them. In spite of his being overweight, he jumped nimbly from the boat onto the muddy bank.

"Hey! My friends!" he said and hugged all three. They slapped at each other's shoulders; they laughed and poked at John and then led us into the house where the boat boys were already busying themselves clearing and repairing space to set up our sleeping and cooking equipment.

Later, Urbanus sat on the floor with us. He said he had been staying in what was left of his house. "We tried to bring all the people of the other villages back with us so we could all live peacefully, without fear of the government," he said. "We took sago and tobacco and fish and went up the River Topap to where the people of Kapi were settled. We told them that it was time to go back downstream to our homes.

"But the men were angry. 'What do you want here?' they said. 'We are all right and do not want to go back!'

"They beat us and chopped up our canoe with their parangs. They let us stay the night and in the morning they gave us a broken dugout and we came back here."

Urbanus seemed restless and tense. He squatted with his elbows on his knees, shifted from one foot to another, sat cross-legged, and kept turning his head to look at the other men as if he did not know how much to say or had already said too much. I knew he was afraid we would ask about the killing of the four Indonesians at the mouth of the Owap River, men who had been killed earlier that year, possibly by Asmat from Ao.

Urbanus had closely cropped hair in a Western sytle which emphasized his high forehead. His cheekbones protruded and his jawline was square. I had not recognized him at first since on earlier visits he had had long knotted hair. There was no way of knowing his exact age. He looked to be in his forties but must have been at least ten years younger, for his father had once told him that he had been born soon after the two unexploded Japanese bombs had fallen on Asmat.

Urbanus's lips twitched nervously as his eyes darted from me to the other men before focusing again on John. "We, the people of Ao, had decided," he went on after a while, "that Tuhan Jesus would save us if we returned from the River Topap. We prayed to Him for help. We wanted to see the camat at the army post in Erma to tell him that we were back, even though we were frightened of what he would do to us. We left the jungle and spent the night here. We prayed again to Tuhan Jesus. In the morning, we saw a canoe on the river and were certain it was the soldiers come to kill us. We took out our weapons but we saw that we were wrong, Pastor. The canoe was not full of soldiers. It was full of our own people who had followed us down the river. We hugged one another and were happy because we were sure then that Tuhan Jesus was on our side."

John, impatient to learn everything as quickly as possible, sat forward in his folding chair and mumbled in his Minnesota accent, "Shit, man! Get on with it!"

"Then we went to the post." Urbanus shivered in memory of that day. Gooseflesh appeared on his chest and arms. "We were frightened. The army surrounded us and took four of us prisoner. The others were sent back to get the rest of the men and women and children. The camat shouted at them that they must return the next day or the four prisoners would be killed.

"Pastor knows how far it is to the River Topap. There is no way to go up in one day. It takes two days to reach the bivouac when we paddle with the water and the people all left with the water going down. Then there is another day for the return. We prisoners knew this and ran away. We knew they could not come back the next day. We did not want to be killed, so we ran away. The army men were sleeping. All night long, we were laughing because it is so easy to fool the Makassar men." (All Asmat think that all Indonesians come from Makassar.)

"The army was waiting when everyone came back to the post," Urbanus went on. "The soldiers stood at the edge of the river with their rifles aimed to shoot. Some shot their guns, but army men do not know how to shoot. We jumped this way, we jumped that way, and we jumped into the river." The three men got up and jumped, hopped, twisted, turned, crouched, and howled with laughter, showing us how they had escaped the bullets aimed at them. "We were laughing and jumping and no one was hurt.

"Then the camat came and the shooting stopped. He kept the men there the whole night asking questions about the killing on the River Owap and who had done them. We told him nothing. We were afraid that he would kill us, but in the morning he let us go home."

We could get no more information then from Urbanus and the others. I wrote a lengthy report for the bishop that provoked him into action six months later when we heard again in Agats that the people had returned to their homesites. We went up in the same mission boat and were joyously welcomed in Ao. White lime was tossed over us from long reed containers. Men and women and children had painted their faces; their hair sprouted white cockatoo feathers. They danced and yelped, and finally lined up one behind the other in orderly fashion to formally shake the hand of each of us.

The long-empty house of the teacher was quickly cleaned out. The teacher himself had gone to Agats when the villagers went up the Topap River and had not yet returned. Men arrived immediately after we finished our supper of rice and canned corned beef. They sat on the floor and smoked tobacco we put out for them.

Although the bishop had not been in Ao for two years, the people remembered him well, respected him, and understood he would always help them.

"Why did you go so far upstream? Why did you come back?" he asked them.

The older men all began talking at once, but it was Urbanus Umu who was loudest. "We came back because we were not happy so far from home. We came back because we were thirsty for tobacco and hungry for fish. We ate sago on the River Topap and on the River Tamai, and sometimes pig meat, but it was not enough, and there was no fish."

The soft voice of Seraipitsj broke in. He was naked and looked stronger, cleaner, and more dignified than any of the other men. There was an elegance in the way he sat, his back perfectly straight, his voice no more than a whisper. The clothing of the other men gave them an entirely different appearance. Nothing fit properly; their bodies did not conform to the shapes and sizes manufactured on other islands, in other countries. They were as if degraded, no longer possessed of the grace and pride with which they had carried themselves in former times. How could a simple piece of cloth so change them? How was it that even I held myself differently when free of all body covering?

To me Seraipitsj, in his reluctance to change his ways, was one of those who represented the whole of Asmat's past, the time when revenge for all deaths was ever present in the minds of the men. He looked at the bishop as if regretting the loss of those times when it would have been normal to fight and kill those who were enemies. "We were very angry, Bapak Uskup," he insisted. "We were angry because we had worked long and hard with the wood and there was no money. Headman Urbanus Umu went to the camat in Erma and the camat said we must wait for our money. Urbanus Umu went again and the camat said to wait. He went again and again, and always the camat said, "Wait. The money is in Merauke."

"We never received money when we cut wood. Two times we cut wood and did not get paid. Camat Rupumbo was always angry with us when we did not cut for him. All of our wood went out on the ship *Isabella* and on the *Darpo II*. Camat Rupumbo said we must also cut wood for the head of the government forestry department. They never gave us anything, only the tobacco before we went into the jungle for them. There were no knives, no axes, no money. Asis came and beat us with his iron belt. He pointed his rifle at us and shot it over our heads when we did not work. They came and made us cut wood. We did not know who they were. They came with their beatings and their guns and took our wood and gave us nothing."

Amatus Dje interrupted. "We were still angry, Bapak Uskup, when Samat came and said, 'Now, each man must cut ten logs of ironwood, all in one week.' Urbanus said it was not possible. We could cut two logs in one week. We might cut three logs, but ten in one week is impossible. 'We are human beings,' he told Samat, 'not machines.' Then Samat lined us up and beat us with the barbed tail of a sting ray. Our backs were bleeding. He beat us and shot off his gun. It was then that Urbanus decided to listen to what the men of As Atat and Nakai had said, that we should go upriver and hide in the jungle.

"Samat went to Merauke but the soldiers stayed here. Borlak was their leader. He was taking our women every night and we were angry. All the army men were taking our women but we could do nothing against their guns.

"Borlak called us together one day and said the ten logs must be ready in two weeks' time at the mouth of the River Fai for the big ship. Then he sent some of us into the jungle to hunt crocodile, even though the government told us that it is forbidden to kill them. Borlak told us to be back in two weeks. The soldiers stayed in the village and we went on alone.

"But we were very clever, Bapak Uskup. Some of us paddled upstream and some paddled downstream. In the night, we met and stayed in our bivouac at the River Potsj. We laughed at how easy it was to fool the Makassar men. We were not going to cut wood for Samat or Borlak and we were not going to hunt crocodiles.

"The next day, we went up to the River Topap. Some went to the River Tamai. We were afraid the government would send a plane to catch us and beat us, so we did not build our houses in one big village, but one house near the river, then another house.

"But, Bapak Uskup, it was not good there. We were not happy. We could not use our weirs. The level of the water did not change every day as it does here. The sea does not move so far inland. We did not know that. The water is high only when there are heavy rains and the water rushes down from the mountains. We had no fish and we had no tobacco.

"We knew that Tuan Silas was nearby in the village of Ndoema, where the men wear penis sheaths and have no canoes or shields. We knew that Tuan Silas was with the OPM."

Amatus Dje used to visit me once a week when he was a schoolboy, attending the Catholic junior high school in Agats. I learned a great deal from him and often heard of this mysterious, almost mythical Tuan Silas, said to be leader of the southern coast of Irian Jaya's group of the OPM (Operasi Papua Merdeka), the Free Papua Movement. His rebels had struck the village of Akimuga two years earlier, killed the non-Papuan Indonesians, and raided their shops. No harm was done to the Dutch pastor there but his radio was taken. Amatus and other Asmat say that the pastor had been instrumental in providing food and medical aid for members of the OPM and had always sympathized with their plight.

"We went to see Tuan Silas," Amatus Dje said. "He told us that we are human beings like other men. We are real people, he said, just like the people of Makassar, like you have always told us, Bapak Uskup. We are human beings and not animals like the Makassar men always say we are."

The people of Asmat have always thought of themselves as the only "real people," the "true human beings," and have considered all others as lesser or higher creatures. The words in their own language for themselves, for their own groups—Keenok, Kawenak, Keenakap, etc.—all literally translate into "real people." They were therefore humiliated when the first Indonesian catechists arrived from the Kei Islands in 1953 and called them animals because they were naked and could not read or write. The catechists said they had come to teach the Asmat how to become human.

People who live downstream or upstream from a particular group and who are not connected through family ties are looked down upon and might even be referred to as "shit-eaters." On the other hand, when the bishop arrived as pastor of the Keenakap

village of Sawa, in the early 1960s, the real people there called him
Ndatipitsj, Spirit Man.

Amatus Dje continued: "Tuan Silas said, 'Irian must advance
like the rest of Indonesia, and Asmat cannot remain behind. We
must go ahead.' We did not understand all he said but he told
us that people from other countries were helping us with money
and guns.

"He showed us a banner. He said it was the banner of Irian. It
was made of paper and had a crown pigeon on it, the symbol of
Irian. There were two hands, one holding the pigeon, the other
holding an arrow."

The bishop turned to me. "Are you getting it all down, Tobias?" I nodded and flipped the pages of my journal, showing him
it was all there, the names, the places, the beatings, the ships, the
documented information he would send on to the government in
Merauke. Within the week, the journal would be filled with almost identical stories told from the points of view of the people of
Kapi and As Atat.

The bishop looked back at the men. "Now," he said in his most
serious voice, "you must tell me about the Makassar men and how
they were killed."

The Indonesians of Agats were terrified that the four Indonesians
who had been killed at the mouth of the Owap River had been
murdered by members of the OPM who were about to attack
Agats. Rumors of murders of Indonesians throughout Asmat
reached us three and four times a day. One widely spread story
contended that the bishop had hidden the killers, together with
the heads of the dead, in the swamps behind the mission and was
feeding them every night.

The army and police were mobilized in Agats, but they were so
frightened of the Asmat that they refused to patrol the walkway in
the dark, even though they had guns. The merchants banded together and marched in small groups around the raised, wooden
walkways every night for a month. Shots were occasionally fired in
fear, but almost certainly only at noises from night animals, the
squeaking flying foxes sailing from coconut tree to coconut tree,

the sad cats that lived in the hospital and roamed the mud in search of rats and small marsupials, or the wild dogs that rummaged through the garbage the Indonesians tossed casually from their windows and doorways. I was forcefully approached one night, returning from the mission after midnight on my way to my own house. My flashlight was shining brightly, an indication, I thought, that I was not a terrorist, but three men suddenly pushed rifles into my face before they turned on their own lamps and recognized me. There were no raids on Agats and gradually life returned to normal.

"Now, tell me how the Makassar men were killed," said the bishop. The men frowned and whispered to one another. The bishop said, "You know me. You know Pastor John and you know Bapak Tobias. You know we will not tell the army or the police anything you say. I only want to know what happened. You have nothing to fear from us."

"Yes, we will tell you, Bapak Uskup," said Urbanus Umu. It was as if the men had long ago decided they must tell the story to the bishop. "We went down the River Owap. We went with Tuan Silas. We did not want to go, but Tuan Silas needed our dugouts. The people of Ndoema have no canoes and cannot paddle, so we took them downstream.

"The people of As Atat had been fishing in the sea and saw the men of Makassar bivouacked at the mouth of the river. They went to them and traded sago for tobacco. When they came back upstream, they told Tuan Silas. He said, 'Let us go and take their tobacco. Then we will frighten them and chase them from our rivers.' It was Leo Akum and Ndatus Djiitsj of Nakai who said, 'Let us kill them.'

"We paddled the men of Ndoema. As Atat paddled and Kapi and Nakai paddled. We were many canoes together going down the River Owap in the night. The Makassar men were in the bivouac at the mouth of the river. It was nighttime and everyone was sleeping. One of the Makassar men was sick and could hardly move. Tuan Silas grabbed his leg and told him to get up. The sick man said, 'No! Who are you to tell me what to do!' Tuan Silas stood there and said, 'I am Tuan Silas of the OPM!' and jabbed his parang into him and disemboweled him. He pulled out the parang and there was blood everywhere, on the bark floor, on the pandanus mats, on the mosquito nets. One of the Makassar men was running away but they shot him with an arrow. It went into his arm and he pulled it out. But more arrows hit him in the chest and in the stomach. He fell down and blood came out of his mouth. They jabbed spears and shot arrows into the other two men and killed them. Two of the bodies were thrown into the river and two were burned.

"The people of Ndoema did the killing. We sat in the canoes and waited. We did not go with them. Later, when it was all over, they called us and we saw the bodies. We saw what they had done, Bapak Uskup, but we did not kill them. We did not take the dead bodies and we did not eat them. It is not true that we ate them. There was no feast. We are Christians now and we no longer eat human meat.

"We took all the goods in the bivouac and hid under the trees. Tuan Silas took the big fishing nets and everything else there. We had some tobacco. We hid in the jungle by the River Topap and stayed there. We were afraid to go back to our own villages. Whenever a plane flew overhead, we were frightened and hid among the trees. We always paddled in small groups because we thought the planes would see us. Now we are back and we are afraid the soldiers will kill us."

FIFTEEN

"WE have been talking and we have been talking, Bapak Uskup," said Urbanus Umu to the bishop. "Now, it is enough. Now you must tell us a story."

The bishop looked at me, raised his eyebrows, and said, "Well? What about 'The Three Little Pigs'?" I had often heard him tell biblical stories and fairy tales from his childhood that he narrated like Asmat myths.

"Great!" I said, and wondered what he would make of it.

It was already after two in the morning according to the bishop's watch, but the men in the room were still as animated as they had been several hours earlier.

Dressed only in a pair of scarlet red shorts, splotched with the white lime that had earlier been thrown over us in welcome, and smudged with soot from the fireplace, the bishop wiped perspiration dripping down his face. His belly, sparkling with scattered drops of sweat, bulged below the greying hair of his bare chest. He sat cross-legged, leaning against the few gabagaba slats, sections of leaf stem in the wall. He sat among the Asmat as if he were one of them, almost a red-haired albino with brown eyes. He turned his head and looked around at those sitting with us on the floor.

The older men were naked; the tattered shorts and shirts the younger ones wore gave them an impoverished, degraded look. A shell nosepiece curled through the septum of an old man whose sunken cheeks were cross-hatched with fine, shallow wrinkles, like caked mud at the river bank when days have passed without rain. In the nose of another old man a human bone projected, carved with the root design of a banyan tree. Sacred in Asmat, that tree absorbed

141

the evil of women who had died in childbirth, whose bodies were left to rot in its twisting branches, far from the village.

Decaying beams of the house exuded a fetid air which, with the sweet smoke of spiced tobacco and the heavy smell from the bodies of the men, combined in an atmosphere of companionship and calm.

"*Tare atakam,*" the bishop began in Asmat. "In olden times," he said, articulating each syllable slowly and carefully, "there lived a man and a woman. The man was called Sosoktsjemen and the woman was Tsjenakat." Names such as "Black Penis" and "Good Vagina" are common in Asmat.

"Sosoktsjemen and Tsjenakat lived a long time ago. It was the time of our ancestors, the time of the Creator, Fumeripitsj, when he was still using bone tools and shells to carve figures in his great feast house.

"Sosoktsjemen and Tsjenakat were living far upstream," he went on, stretching out his left arm and into its armpit noisily slapping his right hand to indicate great distance. "They lived on the River Paii, at the second bend, before it enters the Djirep, where spirits dwell in the whirlpools." The bishop spiraled his arm. The men understood his gestures because they were their own. His stories always had characters from Asmat itself.

The men humped forward a buttock at a time, their heads leaning toward the bishop as if to deepen their concentration. "Sosoktsjemen and Tsjenakat had three children. They were called Umpu, Wu, and Sanau. They were very young and had not yet been given their proper names. Sanau, the youngest, had only recently received a name for the first time, the day he began to walk, the day Sosoktsjemen and Tsjenakat decided he was really human. Not even Umpu, the eldest, had had his nose pierced yet, though Sosoktsjemen was saying the time was near.

"Sosoktsjemen and Tsjenakat were not good parents. They kept almost all the food they gathered for themselves. Unlike other mothers and fathers, they shared little with their children. Only rarely did they bring them sago or other food. Umpu, Wu, and Sanau were hungry all the time. They spent their days at the bank of the river searching in the mud for food, even though Sanau could barely walk and was still learning to dig for crabs and mussels and shrimp. In times of high water he had to stay at home or he would drown. He was already able to stand in the canoe and even used the tiny paddle Umpu had made for him, but he was not yet able to swim properly.

"Sosoktsjemen and Tsjenakat would go deep into the forest and laugh and have sexual intercourse for days at a time, forgetting all about their children.

"Sosoktsjemen took his stone axe, his bow and arrows, his fishing spears, his spears for cassowary and wild pig, and his spears for birds. He took along his dog Ser, named for the *ser* fish he liked to eat. They took fire and the tongs for turning the balls of sago. They took bamboo knives and net carrying bags and carrying bags of pandanus leaf.

"In the forest they pounded sago. Sosoktsjemen broke off the outer leaves of the palm tree and made holes in the trunk to test the sago. The sago was good and he chopped down the tree with his axe.

"Sosoktsjemen took moss from the tree and rubbed it into his armpits, over his anus, and under his testicles. Then he put the moss in the hole in the tree so that the spirit there would recognize his smell when he began chopping into it and would not run off and leave the sago inedible.

"Sosoktsjemen stood close by Tsjenakat. He kept his spears and his bow and arrows in his hands and watched carefully for enemies. He did not want his flesh eaten and he did not want Tsjenakat captured or killed.

"Tsjenakat washed and rinsed the sago." The bishop twisted his clenched fist in opposite directions, imitating Tsjenakat's movements with the sago pith. He pursed his lips and loudly sucked in his breath as Tsjenakat kept in close contact with the tree's spirit. "She squeezed and strained the liquid into the trough she had prepared.

"When this was done, they built a bivouac from the leaves of the sago tree. Tsjenakat went inside to build her fire and to prepare the sago the way Sosoktsjemen liked it. She was a good wife, always making his food properly and never refusing sexual intercourse with him, as some wives do when angry."

The bishop paused to light a cigarette. The men had been concentrating so intensely on the story that they had forgotten to smoke. Now, one by one, they reached into the center of the circle to the small mound of tobacco on the floor. The younger men rolled the tobacco in nipah leaves; the older ones filled their decorated pipes of bamboo. Someone picked up a small stick of firewood, its end glowing, and from it the men lit their tobacco. The pipes were handed from one to another of the older men, each one holding the bamboo tightly against his lips, inhaling deeply and expelling the smoke in a loud puff of satisfaction.

The story had obviously begun well, for the faces of the men were increasingly alert as they became involved with the protagonists. They listened to and watched the nuances of expression in the bishop's voice and face, their mouths open, their breath held or panting in anticipation, their eyes shining with the reflected light from the pressure lamp above us.

"In the morning," the bishop continued, "Sosoktsjemen took his dog Ser to hunt wild pig and cassowary, and Tsjenakat went fishing. In the evening, after a successful day, they filled their stomachs with meat and fish and sago, saving only a small portion to be eaten in the house on the River Paii. They were greedy and preferred to keep most of the food for themselves."

Urbanus Umu clicked his tongue in exasperation at this kind of avarice. The other men shook their heads in agreement. The Asmat always share their food with their families.

Again, the men moved forward on their buttocks. A wind came up and rain pounded on the attap roof. Water poured through a hole above the bishop. Two men quickly adjusted the leaves to stop the leak. The wind swept rain through the open doorway and we all moved to a drier spot. Cigarettes and pipes were relit before quiet settled in again.

The bishop shook his head slowly. "Alas. Sosoktsjemen and Tsjenakat never took their oldest son Umpu into the forest, although Umpu could have helped watch over his blood-mother Tsjenakat in case of attack and he could have helped pound the sago. But they never took any of their children with them, even though Sanau was still sucking milk from Tsjenakat's breast when she wasn't too busy gathering firewood or cooking or fishing.

"All this time, the Great Spirit from the whirlpool in the River Paii was watching and was angry. 'What is the matter with Sosoktsjemen and Tsjenakat?' cried the Spirit. 'They are not good people. They are too greedy and I do not like them. They must be taught a lesson.'

"The Great Spirit said, 'I know. I will change the children into pigs.'

When Sosoktsjemen and Tsjenakat returned from the jungle, they called out, 'Umpu! Where are you?'

"They called out, 'Wu! Where are you?'

"They called out, 'Sanau! Where are you?'

"But there was no answer. The dog Ser was barking even though he only barked when strangers were close. Sosoktsjemen and Tsjenakat pulled their canoe up onto the bank of the river.

"They went into the house and were startled when they saw three little pigs sitting there. The pigs were sitting around the fire, cooking sago as if they were human beings.

"Sosoktsjemen and Tsjenakat were angry and kicked at the pigs. 'Get out! Get out!' they shouted. 'What are you doing in our house? Why are you eating our food?' They kicked at the little pigs again and beat them.

"The three little pigs cowered and squealed, 'But we are your children! Just look at us!' But Sosoktsjemen and Tsjenakat would not listen.

"'Look at me!' insisted the largest pig, standing on his hind legs with his hooves on his hips. 'I am Umpu!'

"'And I am Wu!' declared the second pig, thumping his hoof against his chest.

"'And I am Sanau!' squeaked the littlest pig in his tiny voice as he wiped away a tear rolling down his cheek.

"The three pigs huddled together and stood with their forelegs around one another's shoulders and shouted, 'We are your children! Do not kick us out. We have been changed into pigs by the Great Spirit!'

"Sosoktsjemen and Tsjenakat would not listen. They were very angry. 'Get out!' they howled in their fiercest voices. 'We don't want you. We want our children, not pigs like you!'

"Sosoktsjemen and Tsjenakat wailed and threw themselves into the mud at the edge of the River Paii, as if their children were dead. They rolled in the mud in mourning and rubbed the mud over their bodies. They took their bride-price stone axes from their hiding place in the house and went outside. They ran around and around, carrying the axe blades on their shoulders. They went inside the house again and sat there and wailed throughout the night. The little pigs, terrified of the darkness and the spirits, curled up together beneath a great jackfruit tree and cried and cried and hardly slept at all.

"The next morning, the three little pigs were hungry. They went into the forest for sago, carrying in their hooves the stone axes of Sosoktsjemen and the sago pounders of Tsjenakat. They stood in the canoe and paddled upstream until they came to their sago grounds. They pounded sago and cut nipah leaves and built a bivouac. They sat by the fire and roasted balls of fresh sago. The sago was good and the little pigs were content. They slept well that night.

"But, wait!" said the bishop in a low voice, almost a whisper. He frowned and grunted and made a slithering movement with his upper body. "Nearby was Mbatsjipitsj, the great crocodile. He was in the water beneath the leaves under the banyan tree. He was hiding between the roots of the tree, waiting for just such a moment. Mbatsjipitsj had seen the little pigs going into the bivouac. He smiled to himself and said, 'Aha!'

"Mbatsjipitsj was hungry. He was always hungry. He swam silently up to the bivouac and put his head inside. He opened his mouth, quickly gobbled up Umpu, and disappeared. Umpu was the biggest of the three little pigs and Mbatsjipitsj just opened his mouth and gobbled him up before anyone knew what happened.

"Wu and Sanau looked and looked for Umpu but could not find him. Mbatsjipitsj was no longer there. He had hidden himself again by the banyan tree.

"'Umpu!' Wu and Sanau called out. 'Umpu! Where are you, Elder Brother?'

"'M-m-m-m-m,' Mbatsjipitsj was moaning to himself. He was resting after his good meal and was almost asleep.

"Suddenly, from the belly of Mbatsjipitsj, a tiny, squeaking voice cried out, 'Help me! Help me!'

"Wu and Sanau could hear the voice and knew it was Umpu. For them, Umpu was already dead. They jumped into the mud and wailed. 'O-o-o-o!' they wailed and rolled over and over in the mud. Soon, they were as white as lime with mud.

"'M-m-m-m-m,' said Mbatsjipitsj when he heard them. He was still tasting Umpu, but his mouth watered at the sound of the voices of the two little pigs.

"Umpu cried out again, 'Help me! Help me!'

"'But Elder Brother,' said Wu, 'we too will be eaten if we try to help you.'

"Sanau said, 'Ha! Umpu, I am not afraid. I will help you.'

"Sanau went straight up to Mbatsjipitsj with his stone axe raised to strike him but Mbatsjipitsj opened his mouth and gobbled up Sanau together with his stone axe.

"Wu saw what happened and jumped into the mud. He rolled around and cried and wailed, 'O-o-o-o-o!' He was covered with mud from his little peaked ears to his little curled tail.

"Wu looked at the great Mbatsjipitsj and ran into the forest. There he found a large sago tree, and began to cut it down with his stone axe. Later he sat in a bivouac and ate his sago. Then he stretched out and went to sleep.

"'M-m-m-m-m,' said Wu, moaning with contentment.

"Wu stayed in the forest and lived there many years. He learned to fish and do all the things he would have done had he remained in human form. He married a wild pig in the forest and had many piglets. He never saw Sosoktsjemen or Tsjenakat again. He forgot them and the ways of humans and was very happy."

*   *   *

The men of Ao smiled their satisfaction at the resolution of the tale. Stories in Asmat always end abruptly, always at odds with the manner of Western stories.

Urbanus Umu said, "Good! It was clever of Wu to run away and save himself. Sanau was stupid to think he could help Umpu all by himself."

Exclamations of approval came from all the men.

"Bapak Uskup always tells good stories," said Seraipitsj, addressing the bishop.

The men said to one another, "The stories of Bapak Uskup are always good. His people are like Asmat, the real people."

Seraipitsj, looking like the great war chief he was, sat directly in front of us. His chest and shoulder muscles were hard and youthful. He held himself erect and proud, naked but for a thin neckband of rattan and the bands on his wrists and forearms. He knew himself to be superior to all men because of his fierceness and success in battle.

"I, too, would have run away in the face of the gigantic Mbatsjipitsj," he said. "Wu was the only clever one in all the family. Sosoktsjemen and Tsjenakat were bad. They knew they should share their food with their children. It was right that the Great Spirit should change the children into pigs and that two of them should die. Now there will be no one to help the parents when they are old and sick, when they are too weak to find their own food."

The bishop stretched out his legs, stood up and yawned, indicating it was time for sleep.

Seraipitsj reached into what was left of the tobacco and divided it carefully, apportioning it according to the importance of the men. They all left then to spend what remained of the night with their families.

Chapter

SIXTEEN

AFTER a breakfast the next morning of fried chicken eggs and Spam, John, wearing a white undershirt and tan shorts, stood in the doorway of the house in which we'd spent the night and blew the bamboo horn announcing that services would soon begin. Then from his aluminum patrol box he took out his vestments. He put on the clean white alb and red cincture, and then his red stole. Ordinarily he would have dressed inside the church, but the dilapidated condition of its floor made arranging his formal attire there difficult. The bishop donned his own ceremonial garb of red and white batik, recently made by the Sisters in Agats, and held his folded red and white mitre under his left arm. Barefoot, we climbed down the log ladder, one after the other. The bishop carried his polished, black shoes in one hand and with the other, like John, lifted the skirts of his alb high above the deep mud.

It was raining. Amatus Dje held an umbrella over the bishop's head. John and I carried paper parasols and our thong sandals. Some of the men and women who wore oddments of Western clothing also wore rain capes of pandanus leaf that covered them from head to calf, but most of the parishioners ignored the weather. Sticks and thin logs had been laid down in the thickest of the mud but they were slippery and mud splashed in all directions as the people tread on them.

Bishop Sowada and Father Fleischhacker, stately in attire and carriage, walked slowly and easily along, elegantly holding up their skirts while grandly balancing themselves on logs, but occasionally sliding through mud and splattering their ankles and skirts without loss of dignity. On the porch of the church, water in plastic buckets allowed all to wash their feet before entering.

There was no flooring inside the church, only beams on which laths of bark had been tied. Men, women, and children squatted on their haunches or sat with legs crossed or dangling. Many of the men wore shorts that left their buttocks bare or their genitals exposed. Some women wore remnants of dresses but most wore the Asmat skirt of sago frond.

John set up a makeshift altar by covering two aluminum patrol boxes with white cloth edged in gold. He took out the paraphernalia of Mass and lit a candle. Services began in the Indonesian language. Children sang and young men stumbled clumsily through readings.

After a while the bishop got up, stood still a moment, and looked around. For some seconds there was complete silence. Not even a baby was crying. Then he began his homily.

"Maybe you think that Christ is against you. Maybe you think that I am against you."

Poised, though straddling the empty space between two beams, the bishop was comforting, attractive, engaging, and even, I hesitate to say, seraphic. He spoke quietly, in a mellifluous, calm, eloquent, Ciceronian voice.

"Maybe you think that God Himself is against you because you ran into the jungle. Maybe you think that Pastor John too is against you.

"You cut wood and received no payment. You cut wood many times and received no payment. It is not right. They are wrong. It is not you who are wrong.

"You were not wrong to run away. If I were living here, if I, the Bapak Uskup whom you all know, if I were here and this happened to me, I, too, would run away.

"You went to the camat and asked him for your money and have not received it. These men who do not pay you are bad. It is not the government in Merauke that is bad. The government says you must be paid and I say you should not cut more wood until they have paid all they owe you.

"Do not forget that the Makassar men are afraid of you. They are afraid because they have heard the old stories of Asmat head-hunting. They have their guns and their planes but still they are afraid. They did not go after you in the jungle when you were living on the River Topap. They know you can kill them and hide. It is good that they are afraid.

"I cannot live by myself in the jungle. You know that. Where would I find my food? How would I cut down the sago trees? How would I make fire? The Makassar men, too, cannot live there without you. They, too, need the Asmat. In the jungle we are outsiders and are like newborn babes. We know nothing and you know everything.

"Pastor John and I have been coming here for ten years and we have always told you that you are human beings. Tuan Silas has told you this too. The Makassar men come and tell you that you are animals and they force you to cut wood and they do not pay you. But you are human beings, not animals. I sometimes think to myself, I ask myself, what would happen if you went into *their* forest and cut down *their* trees in Makassar and Java? What would they do? What would they say?"

I was sitting uncomfortably on a beam with my legs hanging down, listening intently as the bishop spoke sometimes in Indonesian, sometimes in Asmat. I looked at the members of this ecclesiastical unit in the bishop's diocese and wondered what the people thought. They had come to know the bishop and their pastor as men who could help them, but none of the women and few of the old men understood Indonesian and were restless. Babies cried and some were soothed with breasts pulled out through armholes of tight-fitting dresses or up through narrow neck openings. Men, too, sat with babies in their laps, sometimes with a finger inside a vagina to calm an infant's nerves. At times babies were held out at arm's length to let them urinate, the stream splashing noisily onto the mud below. Those who fidgeted most, both men and women, stepped from beam to beam, bent slightly forward with arms behind them, holding their children against their lower backs and rocking them up and down. Dogs wandered, sniffed in corners, and relieved themselves more noisily than children.

"I do not tell you to fight the soldiers," the bishop went on. "It is wrong to kill. You could kill them but then you would have to live always hidden in the jungle. They have many soldiers and many guns in Merauke and in Jayapura. If the merchants do not pay you, if the camat does not pay you, you can go again to where there is sago upstream. I know there is not enough fish and you get thirsty for tobacco there, but you must always be strong and you must always stay together."

The bishop paused, walked along a beam, stepped over to another beam, and then walked back. "I want to tell you a story that Pastor Virgil of the village of Atsj told me. He was reading this story and then he told it to me. It is about real people in a village like Ao, in a big country that is called Africa.

"The people had a headman who was sick and dying. He was an old man and had been headman for a long time. The people were mourning for him, crying out that there was no one to lead them when he was gone. Everyone knew he was dying. He, too, was sad.

"He went around the village gathering sticks. He called the people together and took up one of the sticks. He said, 'Look here, my people. Look. Sometimes one of you goes away. He goes to the city and he meets fine people. Everything there is new and exciting. The people of the city look at him because he is strange. He does not look like them and is wearing his country clothes. He stays there and he works but he is unhappy. He is nobody.'

The bishop held up a stick for all to see. "'He is like this stick,'" said the old headman. He held the stick between his hands and snapped it in two. He threw the pieces to the ground.

"'He is weak like that stick,' said the old man. 'It is easy to break a single stick,' he said.

The bishop picked up some more sticks and tied them into a bundle with rattan. "'But, listen,' said the old man. 'Listen. If you stay together, you will be strong. All of you together will be strong like this bundle of sticks.'"

The bishop held up the sticks and tried to break them. He tried to break them with his hands, he tried to break them across his knee. He bent down and tried to break them across a beam, but the bundle remained intact.

"'If you stay together,' said the old man, 'you will be like this bundle of sticks. Nothing can harm you. It is only when you are apart, when one goes this way and another goes that way and there are only a few of you together that you become weak. Remember that you must stay together.'"

There was murmuring among the people as the bishop stepped from one log to another and then sat down. John got up to celebrate the eucharist. Altar boys brought in the paten and chalice and set them on the altar. John took up the paten and, in Indonesian, said:

> He took the bread and gave you thanks.
> He broke the bread,
> Gave it to the Disciples, and said:
> Take this, all of you, and eat it:
> This is my body which will be given up for you.

John held up one of the wafers between the fingers of both hands and displayed it to his parishioners, then put it back on the paten. He genuflected and continued:

> When the supper was ended,
> He took the cup.

John took up the chalice and went on:

> Again He gave you thanks and praise,
> Gave the cup to his Disciples, and said:
> Take this, all of you, and drink from it.
> This is the cup of my blood,
> The blood of the new and everlasting covenant.
> It will be shed for you and for all men
> so that sins may be forgiven.
> Do this in memory of me.

*   *   *

At last the men, women, and children who had been baptized lined up to eat of the bread. John held out the paten with each of the wafers broken into several pieces. All stood humbly with palms together, waiting their turn. I remembered myself two years earlier inside the small private chapel of the monastery in Agats, reserved for the Crosiers and for an occasional Catholic visitor from the West. It was either Trenk's tenth anniversary in the priest-hood or his tenth anniversary in Asmat. On special days— birthdays or anniversaries such as this one—I was invited to evening services.

I had no compunctions about attending. The atmosphere was conducive to reflection and, usually, special care was taken with the readings to avoid any reference in the New Testament that might in their eyes be offensive to me. The songs they chose spoke mainly of brotherhood and peace. There were no crucifixes hanging on the walls, no painted effigies of Mary or Jesus. It was a simple room with chairs and altar.

Before Mass, I stood in the group close by the altar to receive the Embrace of Peace. Normally, after I had embraced each man in turn, I would sit down during Mass itself, but Trenk, who was officiating, checked me with a movement of his hand. A few minutes later, when he offered the wafer, I hesitated and stepped back slightly. "Come on, Tobias," he said, looking me straight in the eye. "It's no different from the matzoh at the Passover Seder." He put the wafer in my mouth and I shuddered. Was that thunder I heard? Or was it my father turning over in his grave?

In Ao, Seraipitsj stood awaiting his turn. I watched him solemnly take the wafer and put it into his mouth and then return slowly to his place with head bowed, hands together in front of him. His body had settled itself into a posture of humility and self-effacement. Where, at that moment, was his virility? Was he, there in church, at the apocalypse of all his centuries of learning, of all the life around him? What could he make of this ritual of symbolically eating the body and blood of Christ? Where now was the man who had fought fiercely in times of warfare and had eaten the real flesh of real men?

On the way back to the teacher's house, Mbanetsjem, in muddy trousers and bare feet, walked with John. I walked two or three paces behind but could clearly hear him say, "I must kill her! I must! She killed my son Asemenam and his spirit will always come back if I do not take revenge."

John said, "But Mbanetsjem, you know that is not true. Asemenam was sick and he died. There was no magic. Tell me again what happened."

"Pastor, it is not right. My boy was good and he was always helping me." Mbanetsjem had smeared mud on his shoulders and sago flour on his forehead. He wore a cuscus fur headband from which hung pieces of broken shell, coix and abrus seeds, and cassowary quills. "It was only two days ago that he died. Asemenam was fine. He was sitting by the fire and my brother's wife Tapnam had just had her baby girl and had come home. She was still bleeding and the blood fell on my son. His skin got hot then and in the morning he died. He was not sick, Pastor. Tapnam killed him with her blood because she was jealous that I had a boy and she had a girl. There was no magic to stop her. Your medicine would not have helped him. Now I must kill her."

"But Mbanetsjem, you know that magic does not kill anyone. I have been telling you for a long time and telling you too that it is a sin to kill. Asemenam got sick from malaria and you did not come to me for the medicine. He was very young and needed the pills. It was not Tapnam's magic that killed him. Do not blame her."

"Oh, yes, Pastor! She did it! Tapnam killed him and I will take revenge!" Mbanetsjem suddenly ran off toward the jungle.

"Bastards!" John barked at me. "Won't they ever learn?"

A line of grownups, adolescents, and children was forming outside the teacher's house, waiting for John's pills or shots. Those with lesions of framboesia, yaws, and running sores uncovered their buttocks and John placidly injected penicillin; malarial patients received their doses of cholorquin with instructions of when and how many to take; headaches, backaches, pains of all kinds were treated with aspirin, and cuts and wounds were stitched, painted with iodine, and bandaged roughly but with skill.

We lunched as usual on rice and canned corned beef with ketchup and the small chilies hot enough to please the strongest tastes, grown in Asmat by teachers from other islands. We napped, showered indoors with buckets of water carried from the river, sat in our chairs, and gossiped.

"Everyone in the village called him Don Juan the Catechist. He was sleeping with just about every female of every age there. I said to him, 'Don't you know that's morally wrong?' 'Why should it be wrong?' the catechist asked. 'They are not baptized yet!'"

We drank our Johnny Walker Red and suppered on sago pancakes with peanut butter and jelly. I suggested that one day we really must try the Soup a la Cantatrice recommended by Isabella Beeton in her *Book of Household Management*, published in London in 1861. Miss Beeton's recipe called for sago flour, eggs, sugar, a bay leaf, and beef stock. According to Miss Beeton, the soup "had been partaken of by the principal singers of the day, including the celebrated Swedish Nightingale Jenny Lind." Maybe sago soup would improve the voices of the children in church.

Some men, including Seraipitsj and Urbanus Umu, came in. They sat and smoked. The bishop said, "We want to hear an old story."

"Seraipitsj," I said, remembering my last visit there, "tell about Amandjanep and Tordjanep."

All the men smiled. It was a story told with variations in almost every village in Asmat. Seraipitsj slapped his thigh and shook his head in pleasure at the thought that I had recalled the names. He was a good storyteller and everyone except the youngest children knew this one.

Cigarettes and pipes had to be prepared and lit before Seraipitsj could begin. Everyone was in a good mood. They had told the bishop and the pastor of having run off into the jungle to escape the wooding and of the killings on the Owap and no one was angry. Even those who did not understand Indonesian had listened to and enjoyed the bishop's homily. The sermon had been talked about all day long and by then everyone knew the tale of the old man and the bundle of sticks.

"*Tare atakam,*" Seraipitsj said, beginning the same way the bishop had begun his "Three Little Pigs" story, the same way all old stories began. "In olden times, there lived two Djaneps, two men with the same name. One lived on the land and one lived in the water. The land Djanep married his own sister. When she was his wife and he was having sexual intercourse with her, just as he was entering her she began to bleed from the vagina. The land Djanep, Tordjanep, was very surprised and very angry. He gathered the blood in leaves and took them into his dugout canoe. Then he and his wife paddled until they came to the River Siretsj and the mouth of the small River Sor. There Tordjanep laid his paddle across the canoe, threw the leaves into the river, and dove into the large, violent whirlpool there.

"Down in the water Tordjanep met another Djanep, Amandjanep, Djanep of the depths. Amandjanep had a large feast house there with many fireplaces. Amandjanep had no eyes and Tordjanep had no asshole. When Tordjanep went down, Amandjanep was out gathering sago worms in his forest. Amandjanep returned to the feast house with the larvae he had gathered. He did not know that Tordjanep was there because he had no eyes and was blind. Amandjanep made fires in all the fireplaces and began roasting the sago worms. Tordjanep, watching this, took the sago worms and ate them because he was hungry. Tordjanep was eating and eating them every day and Amandjanep kept cooking the worms until there were none left. Then he went back to the forest and gathered more. While Amandjanep was in the forest, Tordjanep said to himself, I have been hiding a long time from Amandjanep and eating his food. Today, I am going to embrace him.

"Amandjanep came back with the sago worms and started placing them on the fires again. He went from one fireplace to another. When he finished putting them on the last fire, Tordjanep poked him. Amandjanep was startled and said, 'This must be a man.'

Tordjanep embraced him but Amandjanep jumped back and started to yell, he was so surprised. Amandjanep asked, 'Who are you?' Tordjanep said, 'First you must tell me who you are because I am the visitor and custom says you must talk first.' Amandjanep said, 'I am Amandjanep.' Tordjanep said, 'I am also Djanep, Tordjanep.' They became friends because they had the same name.

"Tordjanep saw that Amandjanep had no eyes, so he said, 'How is it that you have no eyes?' He felt sorry for Amandjanep. In the meantime, Amandjanep had started investigating Tordjanep's body with his hands and noticed that he had no asshole. So they felt sorry for one another. They tried to help each other.

"Amandjanep asked Tordjanep to slit his eyes. Tordjanep took a seashell and slit open the eyes. After that, Amandjanep could see. 'Yuh!' he said. 'Now I can see my friend.' Tordjanep asked Amandjanep to open his back so that he could shit. Amandjanep performed the operation with the same seashell. Tordjanep was lying on his belly with his ass up. As soon as Amandjanep cut into Tordjanep's ass, the shit flew into the air. Tordjanep was very happy.

"The two Djaneps became good friends. One now could see and the other could shit. Amandjanep suddenly saw that he didn't have a hole in his penis and asked Tordjanep to make one there. Tordjanep opened it with the shell and water splashed out like an explosion, gushing over Amandjanep."

By the time Seraipitsj had finished the story we all were rolling on the floor with laughter, holding our aching bellies.

The bishop used my notes and reports together with his own information from other villages, in addition to reports from the Fathers. He sent a detailed account of the manner of exploitation to the head of the central government in Merauke and was later invited to discuss matters with officials there. A flurry of activity took place and it began to look as if there would be a change, but life quickly reverted to what it had been before the reports.

In 1983 the bishop invited a reporter from *Kompas,* a Catholic newspaper in Jakarta, to come to Asmat and see what was happening. The reporter was briefed when he arrived and was then sent out alone to see for himself. He traveled for three weeks and returned to Jakarta to begin a series of articles denouncing the government and merchants for their unethical, immoral, violent behavior, giving details of specific incidents. When the articles appeared, there was a fury in Jakarta in government circles. The Crosiers of Asmat were frightened by the stories and told the bishop he had gone too far, that they could not support him in this—they would all be thrown out of the country and the bishop himself would be shot, just as in 1965 Father Smit had been shot by an official for interfering in the school system. The bishop stood his ground.

Kompas is read by many foreigners. Indonesia was losing face because of the articles. The editor-in-chief was told by government officials that if he didn't stop printing negative stories and substitute positive ones, explaining all the good the government was doing, the newspaper would be shut down.

Officials were sent from Jakarta to Agats to talk to the bishop and to the government there. In Agats they quickly instituted reforms, fired the head of the army and the camat of the area in which most of the wooding was taking place. Loggers received a list of regulations to ensure that the people would be paid as soon as they took their logs to the ship, the price per cubic meter was fixed, a doctor was ordered to attend accidents or anyone who became ill while working, and there was to be no violence or forcing the people to cut wood.

It is difficult to say how long these reforms lasted—two or three months at best. In 1983, when I had finished the museum's card catalogue and was preparing to leave Asmat for New York, the bishop asked me to work with him on teaching the Asmat how they were being exploited. He produced the ideas, while I worked them out with cartoonlike drawings. We did a series of them, each of three or four panels. We put them up in the mission house and invited the Asmat to comment. Had we thought ahead we might have expected that no one would know how to approach the sketches—whether to look at the panels from left to right, from right to left, or from the center to either direction. Nor did the Asmat understand the basic problems we thought we had worked out so carefully. In the cartoon about wooding, the first panel shows a young man chopping down a tree. Behind him is dense forest. An old man stands close by and says, "Are you cutting down the tree to make a canoe?" "No," says the young man. "I am going to sell the wood." In the next panel, the same two men appear, but the forest now has only a few trees. The old man says, "Why are you doing this?" The young man answers, "To make money for tobacco and clothing." In the third and final panel, there are no longer any trees to be seen. The old man says, "If you cut down all the trees, how will you be able to make your canoe? Without your canoe, how can you go into the forest to pound sago and get your fish?" The Asmat looked blank when this was explained to them in detail. There always were trees, there always would be trees, no matter how many were cut down.

More recently, the bishop tried to set up a symposium with the governments of Merauke and Agats, to discuss relationships between the government and the Asmat in the past, what they are now, and what they should be in the future. There were seven postponements as of mid-1985, when the bishop finally gave up.

Chapter

SEVENTEEN

AT daybreak the next morning, the mappi was loaded and we went to spend the next four days in Kapi and As Atat, two other villages whose populations had run off. After we had recorded what the men there told us of their time on the Topap and Tamai Rivers, we continued on to Iroko and Djakapis, places I insisted we visit though neither was properly part of John's parish. They were not far but were remote in having had little contact with the outside world. As far as I know, John and I, and possibly the bishop, were the only visitors to have been there up to that time.

The character of the forest had been changing for days. Moment by moment the changes were almost imperceptible, but in time the nipa disappeared and the variations of prop-rooted pandanus became strikingly clear as brackish waters sweetened and the banks of the rivers were suddenly of sand instead of mud. Stands of sago palm lined the rivers, many in flower, a sign that there was more sago than the people could eat, for once it blooms the tree's pith is no longer edible, only its sweet top.

We saw wild jackfruit trees, more and more of them, clumps of bamboo bursting forth for the first time, banyan trees larger and closer together, their plank roots above ground enmeshed with gray web. The canoe trees and ironwood stood high above the other vegetation, slender betel nut curved upward, stretching above the lower layers of the forest, and rattan in its various guises climbed branches and bushes. Gardens of banana trees and taro had been irregularly planted in rough clearings, and left to grow untended until their owners returned to harvest the yield. Ornamental grasses edged the river at turns, bending under the weight of their feathery blossoms. There were tree ferns and ginger and schefflera that made my heart ache when I thought of their miniature versions in my New York apartment.

Travel was luxurious and relaxing in the mappi, in spite of the clattering, chugging sounds of the motor that made talk almost impossible. We sat and read, looked at the map to follow our progress, wrote in notebooks, watched the passing scene, drank warm beer, ate canned foods and rice. It rained, the sun came out, and it rained again, often so heavily that we rolled down and tied in place the canvas flaps of the mappi to keep ourselves warm and dry.

An ibis swooped across the Momatsj as we turned into it from the Djirep. A white egret flew up, sailed upstream, settled down, flew up again as we approached, moved farther and farther upstream until at last it landed high in a treetop. Downstream, close to the sea, there had been small wading birds and spoonbills and occasional pelicans. Downstream, too, multitudes of white cockatoos had burgeoned like sprays of white petals, while upstream pairs of black king cockatoos cawed, raised their red crests in anger, and hid in shadows.

Far ahead, where the river turned again, the Djajawidjaja Mountains appeared above the forest. A flock of flying foxes, hanging upside down in the trees in which they slept, flapped their wings and flew off to other trees. Coveys of yellow sunbirds, red and blue parrots, white doves with black wingtips and tails flushed up from the foliage, scattered, came together and pulsed like paramecia before coming to rest behind the edge of the forest. Hornbills, one after another, beat the air with their huge wings and soared across the sky above us. The loud sound of their wings gave credence to the first tales from New Guinea told by Portuguese, who thought the sound must have come from rhinoceros thudding through the forest.

The mountains vanished and were visible again at the next turn. I watched the bends of the rivers carefully. On the insides, where water runs slower, short pandanus and masses of tall reed grew, and the bushy small-leaved aura trees in which the fireflies lived; on the other edge, thorned vines of rattan spread over brush and trees, and betel nut palms were silhouetted against the lowering clouds.

I recognized a hillock in front of us. Behind it, against all Asmat tradition, the people of Iroko had built their village. Father Trenkenschuh had once pointed out that the Asmat always established their villages on the outer bend of rivers so that in case of attack they could easily see in both directions, upstream and down. The people of Iroko, however, said they had never been attacked from the south and needed no vista there; it was only from the north that danger lay, from the village of Djakapis, and in that direction the way was clear.

Six months earlier, John and I had been there on routine patrol. We had found the village deserted, the houses no more than heaps of rubbish. We were disappointed that no one was there. The boatman had already turned the mappi around and was headed toward Djakapis when we noticed showers of water sparkling in sunlight further upriver. A canoe was coming downstream with three men standing, paddling toward us, splashing up water to attract our attention. They were chanting and clacking their paddles against the side of the canoe. They waved their hands and sang, "O-o-o-o-o-o-o-o-," and yelped in unison, "Uh! Uh! Uh!"

They came up to the boat, climbed on board, jumped up and down, hugged us. Their eyes were wild with excitement. They yelled *"Isap! Isap! Isap! Isap!"* while running along the deck. Then they stopped suddenly, twitching. They looked to us like demons. *"Isap! Isap!"* they cried again, their cheeks and lips quivering, their bodies shaking, every muscle trembling. They slavered, saliva dripping down their chins, perspiration bursting over their foreheads and chests. The fierce odor of their passion was contagious and I felt myself discharging pungent smells. They wiggled their knees and quaked as if in agony or terror.

"Isap! Isap!" they yelled into our ears until we finally understood they were shouting, "Smoke! Smoke!" in their urgent need for

tobacco. They had remembered the sound of the mappi from our first visit there three years earlier, and had been in convulsions from the moment they heard it again. The rackety sound of the motor had made them break out like Pavlov's dogs salivating at the ringing of the bell. They had lived contentedly for three years without tobacco but the sight and sound of the boat had triggered their withdrawal symptoms. They came out of hiding when they recognized our shapes. They trusted us and knew we had tobacco.

We brought some out but their excited hands could not manage to make cigarettes. A boatman rolled one in paper of nipa leaf. Djit, the headman, took it with timorous fingers, inhaled, inhaled again, and handed it to the man next to him. Other cigarettes were rolled and smoked, one after the other, until the men began to calm down.

Djit chattered incomprehensibly at first but his speech soon became clear, though in his ebullience he repeated everything four or five times. "We heard the sound of the motor! Yes, we heard the motor, Bapak Tombias. We heard the motor. We knew it was Pastor and Bapak Tombias. We heard the motor." They had come out because they knew we were not from the government and would not harm them. Djit said, "Now we hide when we hear the motor because we are afraid of the Makassar men."

Djit puffed rapidly on his cigarette and kept the smoke in his lungs as long as he could. The other two men stared at us, smoked, and said nothing. Djit went on. "The Makassar men came and said we must cut wood and we must build a house for them. We said, 'No, we do not want to cut wood, we do not want you here.' They said they would beat our children. We fought them and they shot their guns. We threw them into the river and ran away and now we live in the jungle. Come! We will show you!"

The men tied their canoe to the back of the mappi and rode in the bow. Djit stretched out his arm to direct us. We rounded one bend, then another, then still another. Finally, on the right bank, we saw five canoes tied up in front of a great black opening in the forest. Men and women were there, jumping up and down and yelping with exhilaration. They climbed over the boat and picked up everything moveable until John bellowed, "Everyone off! Everyone off!"

"Is it far to the houses?" we asked.

"No, no! It is just here," said Djit.

John and I went ashore barefoot, wearing only shorts and cameras. The path led through stands of sago trees with long thorns everywhere, on all sides, wherever you might reach out a hand. There was nothing to hold on to, no branch, no vine, no tree trunk, nothing that was bare of sharp and dangerous prickles, needles, spikes, or spines. John used a branch as a walking stick to balance himself over the thin, single logs. I held onto the shoulder of the man in front of me.

I walked along with a ludicrous sense of anticipation. I felt light-headed and walked on indulging myself with fantasies of what lay ahead. Whatever prescience I may have had was partly suspended in my eagerness to arrive at wherever we were going. It had not been surprising that the men had come out at the sound of the motor, since we were known to them and their reason for making contact was, for the most part, their addiction to tobacco. But that they trusted us enough to take us into the jungle to their hidden village was remarkable.

Nothing prepared me for what was there. Nothing sensational appeared, nothing astonishing or impressive, only that I felt it so, that I had already hurled myself headlong into this small part of Asmat life.

Twenty minutes later the path opened into an immense clearing. Ahead, a jumbled mass of felled trees covered the ground in what seemed complete confusion, except for the log trail that continued over and through the wasteland that had once been a sago forest. Hundreds of trees had been cut down to make way for the extensive site of the new village. Here and there, at random it seemed, small houses like bivouacs rose above the detritus, later I counted thirty-five of them. At the south side of the vast open space a men's house, like a long low wall, undulated over rotting woods. Built on poles, the house sprawled on for over three hundred feet.

As soon as I entered the darkness inside, I began to shake. There was only light and shadow but my heart was pounding, my head too. Through a small doorway, we had entered an almost endless tunnel no more than twelve feet wide, where light was dim and yet intensely defined between black and white. The murky air attacked me, pushed me back, pulled me forward. It was a secret, secretive atmosphere, like entering a passageway into my own being and triggering there memories of an unlived past. The sharply sloping roof gave the walls an arched effect; on the right were doorways, between them fireplaces, sleeping mats, and hanging fronds, all disappearing upward into darkness. There was nothing there, nothing to point to and describe, but it was a men's house like none I'd seen and it took me back to an Asmat time I never knew, to headhunting days and feasts of human flesh.

I was suddenly in Asmat myth, in the midst of the reality of preparing heads for initiation rites, of disemboweling and dismembering bodies to be consumed, in the midst of the desperate brutality and bloodthirstiness of which my friends were capable in their attempt to free themselves from the demands of ancestors who craved vengeance. I stopped just beyond the entrance and turned my head away. I gasped and couldn't look. For more than a moment, I couldn't go on. John was already in the center of the house, but I stood there, unable to focus or move. Something prevented me from continuing, from taking it all in. I was not aware of having seen anything with my eyes, but I knew the *omu* were there, the houseposts too, and the decorated fireplace. I hadn't seen them, hadn't known of their existence, but I felt them, for they had somehow already been recorded inside me. I held up the camera and clicked the shutter three or four or five times, but I knew there was no way to capture what was in front of me, what was invading me.

Again I wanted to separate myself into two people, the one easily, scientifically recording all on film and in journal, the other, the sensitive man, who was beginning to understand the life and mood of the people around him. I handed my camera to John. "I can't hold it steady," I told him. "Please take the pictures for me."

Gradually, step by step, I forced myself to move forward. I was waiting for some new reality to strike me. Whatever I was imagining, John at least would know the truth, for he was seeing with different eyes. I walked on, step by step, and there were the doorposts by the main entrances, the *tempe,* each with a face carved into it, above it the projecting wing, the penis, the *far* they called it there, carved with openwork designs. Elsewhere, *far* meant butterfly. In the center was the central fireplace, its side lined with interwoven rattan; above it, tied horizontally to the central beam, the two long *omu,* their heads touching. Though I'd only read of them, though no Westerners had ever seen them in place before, I knew they were *omu.* "Omu!" they whispered.

It was dark. I took up the camera again, and again it shook in my hands.

I was aching, hurting from some obscure, secluded recess in my bowels. This torment, the conceit of projecting myself into Asmat life, had assaulted me before. I could not quiet myself. I was afraid of losing the illusion, the sense of mystery that held me spellbound, afraid that John would laugh when he looked at me. But John was saying—I think he was saying—"Incredible! I haven't seen anything like this in all my twenty years here!" He was almost dispassionate, moving here and there, examining everything carefully. "Come! Look at this!" he said and snapped a picture.

Even now, I do not know what an *omu* represents.

"Is it a human being?" I asked.

"No," they answered.

"Is it an ancestor?" I asked.

"No," they answered.

"Is it a spirit?" I asked.

"Is it an animal? Fish? Bird?"

"No," they answered.

"What are they then?"

"They are *omu*."

Carved out of light wood, the *omu* were cylindrical in shape, eleven or twelve feet long, partly hollowed out, with two sets of openings along the body at right angles to one another into which sago frond had been stuffed. They were flat at both ends, one end called the belly, the other end the head, the whole incised with designs the men said were butterflies and tongues. The two *omu* were tied head to head onto the beam.

No one could say when the culmination of an *omu* feast took place; it would happen when the day came, when the war chiefs knew the day was right, when the ancestors appeared, when the snake or crocodile or cockatoo said, "Today we begin." But what would begin remains a mystery.

Days later, far down the Momatsj in Erma, Anton Mborok said, "Yes, I saw an *omu* feast in Pupis one time. It was many years ago, when I was young. Pupis was then on the River Djinim. The *dze*, the men's house, was long, very long. It was in the forest. Outside the *dze* was a deep hole filled with *mbi*, water. The men caught a large snake called *bini*. They cut the snake open and cleaned out the guts in this water. The guts were put into a pandanus mat and the mat was closed up and stored in the roof of the *dze*. The other parts of the snake were eaten. In the *dze*, the *omu*, several of them, maybe four, were on the floor on one side, the men on the other side. They were shouting. There was drumming and the men were screaming and shouting and dancing. The next morning, everyone, men and women, went into the jungle for sago worms. When they came back, the women decorated themselves and danced. They brought sago worms into the *dze* and gave them to the carvers of the *omu* who dumped them onto mats on the floor. When all the worms were there, the carvers divided them up among their families. The *omu* were tied to a beam of the *dze* and the men danced all night. A section of the roof was taken off. A young girl came into the *dze* from the far end and climbed onto the central beam. A young fellow came from the other end, also on the beam. In the middle, where the *omu* were, they met and the young fellow began to stab at her anus with his finger. Then all the men jumped up and stabbed her in the ass. They were all shouting and screaming. The young man stabbed his finger into her vagina and blood squirted out. Everyone stopped dancing. The boy and the girl were married. The boy went outside to the hole in the ground and washed himself there. All the men, women, and children washed themselves in the water. The feast was in the jungle, away from the village, but they went back to the village and ate in their houses. They ate the worms and they ate sago, wild pig, and the shoots of the sago palm."

In Momogu, farther up the River Pomatsj, the old albino headman Paiir said, "The *omu* are carved and painted and are brought into the *dze* with dancing and drumming. The *omu* are hidden from the women and children. The *omu* are tied to a beam and the men climb up. The young men and the boys are on top of the beam, dancing and joking. They stick their fingers in each other's asses and take their own penises in their hands." The men around Paiir were gesturing with their fingers and laughing and slapping their thighs. They got up and humped their hips and held onto their crotches as if having sexual intercourse with one another. Suddenly, the noise, the gestures and movements, stopped. There was only silence until someone whispered, "Guru Mateus! Guru!" Mateus, the teacher of catechism, had returned with taro roots from his garden upstream. The men would not talk again. Guru Mateus had cast his deadening influence over them all.

In Iroko that time, with John along, it wasn't possible to get information on the *omu*. Even six months later, when the bishop was with us, long after the feast was over and the bishop was speaking a dialect the men could understand, we could not comprehend what they said. I traded steel axes for the *omu*, stone axes, shields, and drums.

When we left Iroko, the water of the Momatsj was too low for the mappi to go farther upstream. The bishop and I took the outboard and went on alone to Djakapis. We were loaded with axes and parangs, razor blades, the usual goods. I had been in Djakapis before and had seen the shields there, old ones, used, beautifully carved. I had promised the men to return for them.

The men of Djakapis knew we had spent the night in Iroko and were waiting for us. Some had been in the jungle pounding sago or hunting pig but had returned to the village when they learned of our arrival downstream. At the sound of the outboard, they lined the river. When we appeared, they rushed out and mobbed us, splashing up water and dancing around. They pulled our boat onto the muddy bank. The great *hurahura,* the shouting and the chanting, exhilarated us and we, too, shouted and jumped up and down. The moment we put our feet onshore the shields came out, thirty-six of them. The men charged us, packed in around us, smothered us, made it impossible to see anything but the mass of bodies. We forced them back and had them line up the shields in front of the houses so that we could look at them. They made a magnificent display, that long row of war shields, the almost circular head of a rayfish at the top, and the body carved and painted white, red, and black with designs of flying foxes, cuscus tails, and other symbols of great headhunters.

At first there was some order in the trading process. The bishop paid out the goods while I tagged the shields with the name of the carver and/or owner. But all too quickly, everyone was pushing everyone else, trying to get his share of the goods. It was haphazard and frenzied, with shields shoved at us from all directions. I could examine them only briefly, not my usual way, and we took everything that came into our hands.

It was soon obvious to us that there were fewer axes and parangs than shields, and we could see the men trying to figure out whether there were enough to go around. They pushed the shields hard against us and knocked us about. Finally, the axes and parangs were gone and a great mournful wail rose up from the few who still retained their shields.

One of the men suddenly broke away from the others and ran from one end of the village to the other, howling his frustration and rage. He ran around in circles as if crazed, as if he were running amok. He ran into a house and brought out an old parang, screaming furiously in anger. He took up his shield, waved it above his head and yelled at it. He roared and shrieked, snorted, and then cried out with extraordinary vehemence. "Not good enough for an axe!" I think he said to it. "Not good enough for a parang!" he probably shouted. He took up his old parang and chopped and slashed at the shield, splitting it and smashing it to bits. It was in more than twenty pieces when he stopped and looked down. I went up to him, put an arm around his shoulder, and brought him back to the outboard. I gave him tobacco, nylon, fishhooks. He was calm and laughing when we left.

Chapter

EIGHTEEN

IT was not that I dreamed false dreams, in which events took place that had not happened or could not have come to pass. I simply moved myself backward in time, thinking of the past of which Father Zegwaard had written, and thinking into the memories of men who had talked to me and had described their early lives. I have said that I was often two people: one at this moment sitting on the hot aluminum of the mappi roof, staring ahead into sky and river and forest as if they were screens onto which my mind projected imagined Asmat scenes of war and love; the other self below, inside the mappi, eating, sleeping, listening to the bishop and others, writing in my journal. Sitting alone on top in the sun, with the steady constant clack of the motor to lull me, I could go wherever my thoughts took me. The feast house at Iroko had swept me deep into a consciousness in which I was always partly dwelling, one half of me somehow withdrawn into another space. I moved myself forward, I pulled myself back, I bilocated even while with the bishop—my other self seeking the ways of Asmat past, moving inside the writings of Zegwaard, the violence, killings, and decapitations, the heads dripping blood carried into the men's house, the wild cries of exultation, the savage, triumphant celebration of men and women fulfilling ancestors' demands.

Now, however, the first image projected onto the wall of the forest was nonviolent, that of my friend Simni, peaceful, gentle, face deeply lined, appearing sad and grizzled and standing in the doorway of the museum for the first time, trying to attract my attention with an occasional cough. He had looked around nervously when I motioned inviting him in, but he would not cross

the threshold until I got up and went to the door. Then he smiled
and revealed an almost toothless mouth, becoming for an instant a
Rembrandt beggar man. He was the oldest war chief of Sjuru and
was wearing a dirty, torn cap and dirty, torn shorts, like a
wretched tramp or a tattered bag of decomposing flesh. His back
was bent and he shuffled his bare feet on the smoothly polished
ironwood floor, a texture his soles were not accustomed to. Even
so, he retained a dignity that was striking, though without the
power he must have exuded in his youth.

"Some tobacco?" he whispered into my ear.

Inside the museum, he let out an exclamation of surprise.
"*Aduh!*" he said, and continued with expletives as he noted the
size of the rooms and their contents. "*Wé-é-é-é-é-é,*" he said. Still
standing close to the entrance, he surveyed the displays and suddenly walked straight to the syrinx aruanus shells that looked like
tritons.

"Uh!" he said in a shocked voice, and I felt the memories of old
rush through his body. He reached out and put his hand onto the
largest shell, the type he would have worn in the past to exhibit
his superiority as a headhunter. He touched the shell tentatively,
then patted it. He picked it up and put it against his abdomen in
the position in which it would have hung at his navel, tied in place
with a string around his waist. "*Aduh!*" he said. He held the shell
there, then lifted it to his cheek and nuzzled it into his shoulder.
"Aaaaa-aaaaaa-aaaaah!" He cradled it in the crook of an elbow and
stroked it tenderly and whispered, "Ooooo-oooooooo-ooooooo."

We moved around the room and spoke so softly I understood
nothing. He touched the spears, the shields, the objects he recognized as part of his early life, all gone for him now. We sat on the
floor and he emptied the contents of the small carrying bag he
wore on his chest. He picked up the small pipe that Brother Mark
had given him and pinched off a small piece of the tobacco I put in
front of him. He stuffed it into the bowl and lit it with a match.
He puffed contentedly and looked me straight in the eyes, but all
he said was "Tombias," a whisper in a cracking voice that showed
his age, his infirmity, the emotion that welled up in him as he

thought of the past. "Tombias," he said again, a tear on each cheek. He repeated my name a third time and said nothing more. At that moment, I thought the museum had already served its function. After a while, he picked up the shell again and looked at it with longing. He grunted twice as he went out the door.

Until close to his death, Simni visited me once a week when I was in Agats. He came for tobacco and I asked questions in return. I went to see him in Sjuru when he stayed away too long, afraid that he might be ill. He was the oldest man there and must have been in his sixties, old for an Asmat. We often talked of war and headhunting and cannibalism, though my notes tell me that a combination of language difficulties and a lack of experience on my part at that time led to confusion and incomplete information. I had Zegwaard's "Headhunting Practices of the Asmat of Netherlands New Guinea" to guide me, but it was necessary to hear personal accounts as well.

Men much younger than Simni also told of raids and headhunting, but it was always Simni who appeared before me in my visions of myth and war. Zegwaard had used as his informer Warsekomen of Sjuru, a great carver as well as a great warrior, but I substituted Simni for all those characters in myth and reality, no matter what their description or name. Zegwaard had written so vividly that it was not difficult to conjure up the scenes.

It was a time not long ago (at Zegwaard's arrival in Asmat in 1953, warfare was still prevalent). The tale told by Warsekomen was the myth of two brothers, Desoipitsj, the wounded man, who always stayed at home because of physical defects, and Biwiripitsj, the many-colored parrot man, younger of the two, who hunted and gathered food. One day the latter brought home a pig, cut off its head, and pinned it to the floor with a cassowary thighbone dagger. Desoipitsj sneered. "What good is that?" he asked. "Why not replace it with a human head?" "What are you talking about?" asked Biwiripitsj. "Where would I get a human head, anyway?" "Well," said Desoipitsj, "you can use mine." The brothers argued until Biwiripitsj agreed and killed his brother with a spear. He cut into his throat with a bamboo knife and pressed the head forward until the vertebrae of the neck cracked, facilitating the removal of the head. On the floor by itself, separated from the body, the head was still able to speak and advised Biwiripitsj on how to butcher the body properly.

Biwiripitsj made a deep cut with a bamboo knife, starting at the anus, going through one side of the trunk to the armpit, and cutting upward to the collarbone and on to the neck. He did the same thing on the other side, in reverse, from top to bottom. To break the ribs, Desoipitsj said he could use either a palmwood stick or a stone axe. When the ribcage was broken, he put his hands inside the opening and lifted out the organs inside the chest. Arms and legs were cut off, and the entrails removed. All parts of the body were placed in the fire and roasted, although the lower part, including the thighs, had to be mixed with sago in the rolled form of long sticks before it could be eaten. The upper part of the body, arms included, was eaten at once, as it came out of the fire. In this way, Desoipitsj and Biwiripitsj showed the Asmat the way to headhunting and cannibalism.

Imagine Simni and me painting ourselves with white and red and black, giving ourselves strength enough to terrify the enemy. We put our ornaments of human bone and shell through our noses, cassowary and white cockatoo feathers in our hair, loops of dogtooth necklaces around our necks, giving us courage and protection, additional reasons for the enemy to be frightened. Simni paints the three-toed footprint of a cassowary in black on my feet and shoulders, symbols already appearing as magical keloids on his upper arms, to give us the animal's swiftness. We dance in the men's house, sweat streaking the paint on our faces, pouring down our chests, abdomens and legs, the smell of body heat from everyone a power in itself. We eat bitter ginger root and bitter leaves of stinging nettles. We shout and yelp as the men force themselves to the farthest limits of energy and fearlessness. Our skins prickle with cold and our hearts beat faster; we are ready now, almost ready to rush to our canoes and warfare. We sing softly then, so softly none outside the men's house can hear; we sing to placate the spirits who wish us harm, we sing to ask of our brother parrots, squirrels, crocodiles, and cuscus to protect us and help us in the hours ahead. We beseech our ancestors for support and stamina.

We watch the sorcerer rub white lime and leaves onto his right hand. He rubs harder and faster until blood spurts out, a sign that all is well, and a shout goes up from the men. The sorcerer throws up his arms, swings them around, runs blindly from one end of the house to the other, bumps into a man and with a finger makes a slicing gesture across his throat. He takes up a forked bough and together with the war chief stretches it out at arm's length, draws it slowly toward himself and whispers, "Come! Come this way!" And the enemy moves into our trap.

We are warriors; we reach the enemy village before dawn. Silence is broken when one of our group makes a noise. From a house we hear, "Who is that?" When Simni shouts an answer, "It is your husband, Sjuru!" the village is suddenly aware of being attacked.

We of the older group stand back and shout commands. Those with bows and arrows are next, shooting from the distance, while closest are those with spears and shields who rush in to kill. Women and children are screaming and trying to escape, rushing out to the forest in canoes. Men, too, try to escape, but our warriors are fierce and fast. They beat their victims on the head; they tie them up and torture them. The noise is wild and terrifying. Men and women are battered or killed. They scream out their agony, while our men are exhilarated with success, yelping and whooping and savagely striking out at everyone, then focusing on a single victim, beating him, beating her, and then the wails of pain and torment resound excruciatingly in my ears.

I watch as Simni watches, as he calls out orders. His face is placid, though his body trembles. Bamboo horns are blown, blaring out against the hoots, screeches and cries, the intensity of the ruthlessness increasing with the signs of victory. The uproar booms and resonates, shrill and raucous, so clamorous I cannot tell the joyous from the grievous, the celebratory from the plaintive and afflicted. Some pieces of the dead are left amidst the debris of the flesh, only the head and thighs are taken away, torso and arms bloody leftovers. The living victims are knocked about and treated viciously, dragged by an arm or foot to the canoes, seated there in the center, head and hands and chest hanging over a crosspiece. We are on our way home, blood everywhere, the victim in our canoe still alive.

We reach the bend of a river, where whirlpools twist in turbulence and spirits dwell. A man of us stands up and with a bamboo knife cuts into the neck of the enemy in the manner prescribed by Desoipitsj. The vertebrae are broken and the head is removed. The butchering of the body proceeds according to ritual, the knife slicing up from anus to collarbone and neck, continuing on, the arms and legs removed, blood pulsing from the severed arteries, the smell a constant assault on my senses.

We approach our village with horns at full blast to announce the success of the raid. Each canoe has its head and body, each has a horn of a different pitch. The old men and the women waiting on the bank of the river recognize the horn of their own canoe and delight to know a head sits there inside. A ritual dialogue takes place between canoe and shore and the women howl with pride and dance without restraint. We are in the midst of initiation ceremonies and the demand for heads is at its peak.

Simni picks up the head in our canoe by its hair and dips it into the water, lifts it out, and runs to the men's house and pins it to the floor with a cassowary bone dagger. The son of his youngest sister is seated there, an initiate nine years old, watching for the head demanded by the ancestors. The men are chanting "E-é-é-é" and the horns are blowing. Simni weaves a magic mat for his nephew and follows this with other rites: He pours water onto the boy's head and bestows upon him the name of the dead man, scorches the hair of the head and mixes its ash with the dead man's blood. He smears the mixture on his nephew's head, shoulders and body. He covers it all with red ocher, except for the face, which he paints with alternate stripes of white and black. He decorates the whole of the boy according to instructions.

The first night the decapitated head is roasted and put up in the eaves. In the morning, the nose skin is cut off and the jaw removed while Simni says to his brothers, "Oh, this was a good jaw for chewing yesterday, but today it is dead."

With a bamboo knife, Simni cuts from the bottom of the nose, slices up over the head, and on down to the nape of the neck. He tears off the skin and tosses aside the jawbone, which is picked up by a woman who has taken part in the ceremony. He holds the head over the fire so that the flame reaches the temple and back. He uses a stone axe to cut a hole in the side of the skull and shakes out the brains and mucous into a bowl made of sago palm leaf. He mixes the brains with sago, rolls the mixture into long tubes and cooks them in the fire. When they are done, he offers them to the old men and women who eat with great pleasure, knowing this powerful food will lengthen their lives. He keeps the sago leaves and in them wraps the eyeballs and the genitals and hides the bundle away.

Simni carefully fills the nose and eye holes with beeswax, paints the clean skull with charcoal, white lime, and ocher, decorates it with feathers and seeds, and places it at the groin of his nephew, who for three days will sit with the head between his thighs, to absorb through his penis the essence of the dead man, assuring his quick sexual maturity and his development into manhood.

There are other initiates in the men's house, sitting with heads bowed, staring down at the skull between their thighs. Older men sit and smoke, mill around, gossip. Drummers and singers rest. Soon the great room is filled with men decorating themselves, while outside others paint their canoes with vertical stripes of white and red. Simni enters, takes the head from between his nephew's thighs and leads him out to the bank of the river, where other relatives await them. The boy stands in the canoe, the skull below him. He leans on a stick as if he is tired. The relatives are in front. Other initiates are in other canoes. The drummers and singers also enter canoes and the entire flotilla moves downstream toward the sea, toward the setting sun.

Simni's nephew, in our canoe, suddenly becomes old and tired. He leans more heavily on the stick and gets weaker and weaker. Simni offers a shoulder as support but soon even this is not enough. The nephew collapses and lies on the bottom of the canoe as if dead.

Simni lifts the boy and the head, submerges them in the water, then brings them back up into the canoe and removes all the boy's ornaments. The singing and drumming continue as we turn in the direction of the rising sun and the way back to the village. The nephew is lying on the bottom of the canoe like a newborn baby. Soon he begins to move and to crawl on his hands and knees. He stands up and learns to paddle. Back at our village, he goes to our family house and is again decorated. Other ceremonies follow but it is the moment when Simni puts the feathers in his hair, the necklaces and magic bag on his chest, the nose shell in his septum, when he has been decorated once again, that he is no longer a child but has become a man.

Sitting on the hot aluminum roof, ruminating over those images out of Zegwaard that I knew to be true even though Simni, humanist that he was, had not been a great warrior like Serapitsj. I imagined him so and it was enough. There were others to fill that image, Ndotsjemen for one. Aggressive, violent, high in the hierarchy of important men, Ndotsjemen had adopted me as a son during my first week in Asmat. This had been a political move through which he hoped to gain prestige as well as gifts. He flared out in anger at the least provocation and was angry when I had no tobacco in hand to give. He was highly respected by all, more from fear than intelligence or other abilities. He had indeed been an important headhunter and had the skulls to prove it. He had painted and decorated me, had with a shell cut cassowary symbols on my shoulders, too shallow for keloids to form, had given me a skull and named me Sembet. He was never a friend, was always belligerent, laughing in the men's house only when I brought enough tobacco for him to share with his family and partners of exchange. He was powerful of physique and manner, his eyes transfixing with a grave, magnetic look that lured others to his will. He could have led a horde and must have done so many times, a shout from him exacting instant response, the mob following without thought of consequence. He was in great contrast to Simni, who was already dismissed as dead, without voice or influence, no longer taking part in rites and ceremonies except as an onlooker.

It could have been Ndotsjemen, in fact, who said, "We ate them up," but it had been in another place, in the village of Atsj when I asked about the village of Anu. "Oh, yes," Biru had said. "Yes, they came here and we ate them up." We had been talking of Atsjamutsj, a village from which I had just come, where the men had told me of having chased the people of Anu from the River Arowutsj. "They came but weren't here long," said Biru. "We ate up Esin on the River So and we ate Sosombitsjim on the River As. We ate Otsjor on the River Ajip, too. We ate them up."

Chapter

EIGHTEEN

TO the Asmat, the human body is a tree. The human head is the flower and fruit on top, the arms are its branches, the torso is the trunk, the legs its roots. The flower and fruit contain the germinative power of the tree; the human head, their counterpart, has the power therefore to generate growth in the initiate. The seed, magically absorbed through the penis as the head sits at an initiate's groin, brings on his physical and sexual maturity.

The people of the South Casuarina Coast did not have the great raids and headhunting ceremonies of the north and northwest. They had no known rites of passage that demanded heads for initiation, though this was true farther south among the Marind-Anim, where masculinity was stimulated in youngsters by the absorption of semen through sodomy with older males. The Asmat also believe that semen has magical qualities, although conception comes about only from the spirit world. It is, however, only through repeated acts of sexual intercourse that the fetus will grow. Without a constant buildup of semen from a number of different males, including the husband, the child will not grow to its full term and will not be born normal and healthy. In the same way, in the region to the south and east of Asmat, a boy becomes increasingly masculine and grows more quickly as he takes in more and more semen as the passive partner in sodomy. It was thought that the ingestion of semen was necessary to the development of all boys for masculinity, and for all who wished to become great warriors.

For the Asmat, a correlation exists between the seed of the fruit, the germinative power of the human head, and the semen's ability to create a fetus. Although many groups in New Guinea, including the

181

Asmat, considered semen to be a magical substance, it may be that among the Marind it was most widely used in this way. When rubbed onto the body it made the body strong; witches and magicians brewed concoctions to be rubbed onto food and put into drinks to give health to children, relatives, and friends, as well as pain and death to enemies. A combination of vaginal fluid and semen was particularly efficacious and was collected primarily for medicinal use. When spread onto fishhooks, spears, and bows and arrows, it even directed such missiles straight to their targets. Some Asmat of the south mixed semen with human blood and white lime to make a glue with which to seal a lizard skin to the top of a drum, though when questioned the men deny this and refer to its use only among the neighboring Jaqai, Awyu, and Marind.

I traveled throughout Asmat almost from the day of my arrival in 1973, and it never ceased to surprise me that each village had a temperament of its own. No two places were alike; yet there were never specific reasons as to why this should be so. The people of Jaosakor, a village of seven hundred, were sluggish, barely responding to either the Catholic or Protestant missionary. The various clans of Ajam were in constant disagreement with one another and more often than not one or two clans broke away to live in the jungle for a time. Otsjenep was the wildest of the villages under mission control. During the early years, every teacher sent there (under the protection of an armed soldier) was so frightened within the first couple of hours that he (and the soldier) ran back to Agats in terror, without spending a single night there. Sjuru, one kilometer from Agats, visited by every traveler to Asmat, refused to build a primary school, long delaying the education of their children. The people of Manep-Simni had been in the jungle for twenty years cutting wood with little or no payment before beginning to build their first permanent houses. Atsj, with two thousand people in 1983, was growing daily and had a community of Indonesians from other islands who opened shops; they were Muslims and kept themselves completely apart from the Asmat. Some of the differences between villages had to do with the headman or the war chief, some had to do with the missionary there, some with government people and merchants, and some with language and cultural variations. Nothing, however, could explain the essence of a village, why one was more assuring and accepting than another, why one would be belligerent to outsiders and another would take them in. My village was the one in which I felt most comfortable, in which I dared anything and always found sympathetic response.

Only once during my time of wandering did I have trouble of any kind. It happened on the south coast, not far from my village, in a place called Buepis. I was staying at the home of the Dutch Father in Basim who, at that time, was attending meetings in Agats. As usual, I was collecting artifacts and information. Basim had a small sawmill and a shop run by Asmat that was often the destination of people from upstream who brought wood or fish to trade. One day, two canoeloads of men came down the Fajit River with carvings they had made to sell me. I rejected them all as inferior work. The men were furious with disappointment, but calmed when I asked for old skulls. I was aware that, when skulls were wanted, the men normally dug up recently buried skeletons, rubbed the skulls with mud, decorated them, and then sold them to unknowing tourists. These men, however, understood what I wanted.

Three or four days later I went upstream to Buepis in a canoe with four paddlers and two patrol boxes loaded with exchange goods. The entire village was at the bank of the river. Amidst the hoots and yelps, the men lifted me out of the canoe and carried me to the small house of the headman. I opened the boxes to show what I had brought: steel axes, parangs, knives, razor blades, nylon, fishhooks, flashlights, batteries—the things they were looking for.

Several men rushed out of the house and almost immediately appeared at the doorway with a decorated skull. The color of the bone was deep brown, a color not easily faked, for it came from the hair and scalp oils of men who slept on it. The eye sockets and nose hole were filled with resin, job's tear and abrus seeds. The jawbone was connected to the rest of the skull with interwoven rattan that also held a shell nosepiece. A fine net over the top of the skull was a mass of seeds and white feathers. I admired it greatly and said so. I gave the owner an axe, some blades, a knife, nylon, fishhooks, and a plug of tobacco. The men were impressed by my offer and brought in other skulls. Necklaces also appeared, some with the feet of various birds, some with the nippled sections of the chambered nautilus shell, headhunting necklaces of bamboo, of human vertebrae, necklaces of interlaced pigs' tails, and of pigs' penes and scrota, dried and wrinkled with age and still with a powerful odor. I bought armbands of human hair, dance belts of cassowary feathers, bamboo horns, and men's bags. When there was nothing more to buy and I had closed the patrol boxes, a great cry of anger went up from the men.

"You must share the rest of your tobacco with us!"

"What do you mean? I have already given you plenty of tobacco. It is enough!"

"But you still have tobacco in your box! You must share it out!"

"What do you mean, I must share it out? When I came here I gave everyone tobacco. What did you give me? Nothing! I have been sitting here and sitting here and am hungry. Where is my share of your food? Where is my sago? Where is my fish? You gave me nothing and will get nothing more from me!"

The headman took a step toward me and raised a hand. A look of belligerence turned his placid, handsome face ugly. Anger coursed through his whole body, the flesh quivering and exuding perspiration. "Yes, we will!" he shouted. "You must give us that tobacco or we will take it from you!"

I, too, was angry. I called my paddlers. "Bring everything back!" I told them. "Bring back the skulls, bring back the necklaces and the horns and everything else I bought! The people of Buepis are no good and I do not want their things! Bring it all back!"

The men went into shock. This is not what was meant to happen. I faced them and said, "Now, *you* bring back all the money, all the axes, all the parangs. You can keep the tobacco. I will not touch it, after you have defiled it. But I want everything else back. I am ashamed to be here!" Everyone looked at me as if I had gone mad. Could I be serious? "Come on!" I said to the paddlers. "Get going! I don't want to waste more time here. Bring everything from the canoe!"

Suddenly the atmosphere changed. The men began to laugh, hesitantly at first, nervously. They could not believe I would take back all the goods. "It was all a joke!" the headman said. "Yes! Yes!" they all said. "It was a joke. We didn't mean it. *Nder momo, nder momo!* We love you!" They carried me to the canoe and the paddlers took me back to Basim. I was depressed for days and would not move except to eat, even though there were six decorated skulls staring at me from the table in my room at the mission house.

NINETEEN

AKATPITSJIN was the first to open the sexual world of the south of Asmat for me. Some information was already in my head through experience and books, but it took only a few words from him to start in me a train of thought that brought about an awareness of a secret life that was almost certainly unknown to all other outsiders. *"Ndoram ata yima,"* he said to me one night. "I want to balance." The next morning, the use of the word *mbai,* exchange friend, also first appeared.

I had gone around an area of ten thousand square miles before landing in his village. I went there a number of times after that meeting, usually staying in the large house of the catechist and his family, where I could be separate and alone. I kept all my goods there, including my sleeping mat, although I sometimes slept in the men's house at night. The village itself was small, with barely two hundred people. The missionary, the only other visitor, passed through several times a year. The rare tourists went to the larger villages in the area. I liked the place and went down from Agats as often as I could and stayed for days or weeks at a time. Unlike many other villages, it had carvers who were free with information on design and symbolism and who enjoyed answering questions. The character of the people seemed to reflect my own character in ways that even I cannot yet understand. Their only experience with Westerners had been with the missionary, a man completely different in temperament from myself. Yet the people seemed to sense something in me and I in them that linked us together almost instantly. I always wanted to reach out and touch them, and I did, often, although I was frightened that by some premature contact I would lose that first immediate rapport. I hesitated expressing my warmth; I ran my hand over their arms and shoulders tentatively at first, just as they tentatively touched me. The tension between us created an erotic atmosphere that was always on the verge of bursting out into intimate gestures in front of everyone. It was, of course, only with the men that I felt this, though it was obvious that the women, too, would have welcomed physical contact.

I knew nothing of the people when we met at their feast, but I looked at the way the men stood with hand on hip, legs solid to the ground, growing from the earth; I saw the way they laughed, the way they squatted with elbows on knees, hands at chin and cheeks, the way their bodies moved and reacted to the space around them, to each object, human, animal, vegetable. I envied them their easy masculinity.

My first visit was with Father Pietre. We had been invited to an ancestor-pole feast that had originally been arranged to attract a group of tourists who failed to appear. As soon as the invitation reached us, we loaded the outboard with food, tobacco, and other gifts, and raced toward the village. The tide was too low for us to cross the hump of mud that lay in front of that section of the coast; the narrow channel that led into the small river along which the houses were built had no more than a trickle of water. We were prepared to wait for the tide to turn, but no sooner had we stopped than we saw, scattered at the edge of the Arafura Sea, men moving toward us in mud so deep and burdening that their legs sloughed in and out with a languidness that made them appear to be moving in slow motion.

We soon saw the white cockatoo feathers in their hair, then heard the shouts and yelps. A dozen or more men came up, their faces streaked with white and red and black, and splotched with mud. They surrounded us and let out a long "E-é-é-é-é-é-é-é. They pushed the outboard for a mile or more, their chanting easing muscles so that the aluminum boat slipped easily over the slime. The bank of the river was lined with decorated men, women, and children, all dancing and jumping up and down. The drums were beating and some men were singing. We were carried up through a decorated archway and everyone scattered and re-grouped, the women and children outside the men's house, the men inside, then coming out with the huge ancestor poles, raising them vertically with forked branches and planting them in the mud. The carved faces were grotesque, with bared teeth, grinning mouths, noses bearing shells and wooden pins, staring, startled, beady, blank eyes. Carved figures rose one above the other, crouch-ing, squatting, standing, sitting, hugging, some upside down. They were powerful and protecting, surveying the land below, each one different, each one avenging the deaths of relatives. The villagers shrieked and screamed throughout the night, the men finally slumbering at dawn in the men's house, the women and children asleep around the family hearths.

Father Pietre had announced that church services would be held the next day in the old schoolhouse. The muddy room was almost full when I arrived, even though none of the people had yet been baptized. The service lasted no more than ten minutes. The chil-dren were asked to remain for catechism lessons while the adults were cautioned to leave quietly. I went with a group of men to the men's house where the carved poles were stored. The carvings were not traditional to the village and therefore were not to be taken into the sago fields to be broken up so that the spirits therein could be released to protect the trees. The carvers, instead, hoped to sell them to me.

I was sitting on the floor, asking questions and writing answers in my journal, when I noticed that I was being surrounded by a group of men who were lifting me by the elbows, urging me to stand up. They took my arms and legs and held me horizontally at waist level, grunting all the time, "Uh! Uh! Uh!" There were fourteen, all older men, thirty-five or more. Some were naked; others, like myself, wore shorts. They carried me slowly to one end of the long room, turned and carried me to the other end, then back to the central fireplace. The grunting sounds made me shiver. The hands and arms of the men carrying me were hot; perspiration from them slid down onto my own arms and chest. I could look into the circle of faces, all grinning but expressing no mood I could interpret. The man at my right shoulder leaned down and sucked my nose. The grunting continued. The man moved to suck my chin, my earlobes, my fingers one by one. He sucked my nipples, opened my pants and sucked my penis, then sucked on each of my ten toes. My body was not held rigidly, but seemed to be levitating slowly up and down. By the time the first man had passed my head and was at my nipples, the man next to him was leaning over to suck my nose. A third man started, then a fourth, until all fourteen had sucked on all extensions of my body. It was not an erotic experience. Although the men were sucking my penis, I had no erection; my penis and nipples were quiescent. I found myself involved in being the object of a ritual whose purpose was unknown to me. I knew, however, that my smell and body liquids were being absorbed and were becoming part of the men, as if they were imbibing the strength and magic they thought was in me, a magic that would give them not only strength but added prestige that would frighten off the evil spirits of the recently dead. I, in turn, was drawing into my own body their power, ruggedness, the richness of their knowledge and being.

As the men were putting me down and embracing me, I heard the grunting of other men outside, carrying Father Pietre. He was wearing his black robes, stained with perspiration at his armpits and chest. The men brought him up into the men's house, carried him around the room, then stopped in the center. I could not see what was happening, only the bobbing heads of the men bending to suck his nose and chin. *"Tidak! Tidak!"* he yelled. "No! No!" The men finally put him down. He was somewhat ruffled, but the buttons at his neck were still intact, his skirts still unwrinkled.

"I've heard of this ceremony," he said to me, "but I have never seen it. It is a kind of friendship and adoption ritual, but I think it was done primarily to get you to buy the ancestor poles."

Years later I asked Akatpitsjin to explain it.

"Mbi urum, it is called," he said. "We have it when we are

trying to make peace in the village, when we want nothing to disturb the life here. When we suck on your chin and nose and penis and fingers, we take in some of your spirit with the waters of your body. This makes us strong and calms the spirits of the dead.

"It is like when a man dies," he went on, "we suck on *his* penis, too, and we keep something of him inside ourselves, inside the village. We want to get rid of his spirit as quickly as possible before it can do us harm. The relatives put bands of rattan on their arms, on their shoulders, on their legs. The men and the women are together. Drums are beaten from morning until evening. The women are wearing hats so they cannot see what is happening and be ashamed. The men open the women's skirts and suck their vaginas. The women suck the men's penes, too, absorbing the healthy essence that will drive away all evil. Those who are sucked are carried around the house to the sound of grunting, "Uh! Uh! Uh!", a sound we call *omen*. In the morning all the bad spirits are gone."

The *mbi urum* rites marked the beginning of my closest friendships with Asmat men. The fact that they knew me and my body so well gave me the feeling that I was not only close to them but that in the process of their wanting part of me inside them and part of them inside me, we were all being made into a single being, that all our individual characteristics were being combined into a universal concept of life itself. Although this feeling began with the ceremony, it was Akatpitsjin who put it all together, who took me into this world and gave me a sense of myself that liberated me from the neuroses that had originally forced me into my search. I could never know what he or any of the others honestly thought of me, only that they appeared to want me close by and to want to please me. I always referred to the place as "my village."

Akatpitsjin was a handsome man, one of many in the village. His nose was perfectly straight when empty of the shell he often wore through his septum, a decoration that gave him a ferocious look until he smiled and his eyes half closed with humor. The narrow slits above the spiraling shell cast a jauntiness over him that was a delight to see. His upper lip had a scar that in Western cultures might have come from a harelip operation. That, too, gave him a carefree, debonair appearance, the kind of chic a dueling scar on a cheek bestows upon its owner. His ears were small and close against his head. His short frizzy hair seemed to be the same length whenever I saw him, as if his wife trimmed it every other day. The frame of his body was narrow, but daily paddling had given him hard and sinewy shoulder and chest muscles. He held his children in his arms with love and affection, and fed them tasty tidbits—crusts of sago with some of my peanut butter on top, a section of peach from a can I gave him, shrimp, pig meat, even snails he sucked from their shells and offered with his mouth. He was tall by Asmat standards, perhaps five foot eight, and may have been twenty-eight years old. He had five children by the time I left Asmat. When I looked at him fondling his youngest boy and girl I felt a great loss, an emptiness inside, thinking of my father who had never fondled his children and had never shown them any affection. Akatpitsjin's wife was short and still pretty, even after bearing so many offspring. I rarely entered the family house, however, and saw her only two or three times whenever I was there.

One day, a year or so after my first visit, I went there alone and was, as always, greeted with enthusiasm. Akatpitsjin came into the teacher's house soon after dark and invited me outside. He carried a drum and the embers with which to heat the lizard skin top, to tighten and tune it. He beat the drum loudly at first, calling friends. He began a song softly sung. Soon another man was there with a drum, then another, and the three of them played and sang softly. Gradually two dozen or more men gathered and we surrounded the drummers. The men began to sing louder. It was a warm, spontaneous welcome, with Akatpitsjin improvising verses about my arrival and about past visits. The old men and the young were close around me, against me, rubbing my chest and shoulders, my abdomen, my crotch, laughing, playing, running their hands over me. I hugged them and responded, even though I could not recognize individual faces in the dim light of the small fire. The night sky showed the tilted Southern Cross low on the horizon. I looked for Orion and the Pleiades but could not find them. Youngsters of eight and nine were there, too, their arms around the waists of the older men. We swayed and opened and closed our knees in a slow dance. Arms went around shoulders for warmth in the chilling air.

Akatpitsjin finished his song and beat his drum in a rhythm that ended the welcome. The men dispersed. Akatpitsjin came to the house with me, took off his clothes, and got inside my mosquito net. The teacher and his family were asleep behind a wall, in another room. This was not the first time we'd had erotic contact with one another. By then, it was an accepted fact that when I was in the village, he would be spending nights with me.

It was a little later that Akatpitsjin said, *"Ndoram ata yima."* I did not understand the words until he translated into Indonesian: *"Saya mau balas,"* meaning, "I want balance," a phrase that meant nothing to me until he turned around so that we reversed positions and he was on top. It was a startling moment, full of implications I could not then begin to think about.

The next morning, I suggested that we take a walk. I wanted to ask questions without being disturbed by the crowd that would inevitably come to talk and listen and look; I wanted to ask questions that I thought needed privacy.

"Why not stay here?" he wanted to know. I explained, and he said, "Let us stay here. It is comfortable."

We sat at a table and talked. Men and boys came in; the younger ones stood close, leaning their elbows on the table, the older ones sat on the floor. With so many people around it seemed unlikely that Akatpitsjin or anyone else would be making up facts they thought I wanted to hear.

Akatpitsjin always called me *mbai,* exchange friend, but it was only later that I understood the full meaning of the term. There was no secrecy about anything said or done. Everyone knew we had spent the night together, as we had done in the past. I had never

noticed anything unusual in our relationship; it was only Akatpitsjin's use of that phrase of balance and the word *mbai* that started
me questioning.

"Having a *mbai*," Akatpitsjin explained, "is like having a *papisj*
partner, an exchange partner. We all have our *mbai* here. Pastor
has stopped us from *papisj*, from exchanging wives, but we still
have our *mbai*. He does not know this. He knows we have our
exchange friends but he does not know our relationship, and he
does not know the word *mbai*, I think. Before, in the past, two
mbai exchanged wives at mask feasts and at sago worm feasts and
when there was warfare, or when there was so much thunder we
were all frightened. But even though there is no longer *papisj* we
still have our *mbai*.

"Kayet, you know, is my *mbai*, though I call you *mbai* too.
Kayet does not mind; he knows you will be gone soon."

I wondered about Akatpitsjin's *mbai* and what he might think of
our relationship. Akatpitsjin said he was ill and could not go out
of his house, but I thought he might be angry with me and would
not meet me. When he did appear several days later, he seemed
friendly but I was never able to talk to him about the triangle in
which we were involved.

"Kayet and I have played together since we were babies," Akatpitsjin went on. "I found him myself. We found each other. Our
families did not put us together like you think they did. *Mbai*
choose one another and are close, like brothers, but even closer.
When *mbai* are children they play together and touch each other's
penis and examine their entire bodies. They have erections together
and when they are old enough they masturbate one another, they
yipit a minau tamen emefafarimis, they peel back one another's penis.
They do this any time, any place, whenever they feel like it.
Maybe they are out fishing or they are in the forest together;
maybe there is no one else in the house and they are alone.

"Sometimes an older man will play with the penis of a young
boy; sometimes a young boy will play with the penis of an older
man. But it is the *mbai* who have sexual intercourse together here.

Sometimes there is *tamen mbe mbakuman,* when a man sucks the penis of another man, his *mbai.* Sometimes a man enters the ass of his friend, *tamen mbai sumapun,* or sometimes we might say *feper mbimar,* for the same thing.

"We know it is different with the Marind. There are no *mbai.* There are no young men who have sexual intercourse together. There, it is always a young boy with an older man. The boy is given to his mother's brother, who teaches him to cut down sago trees, to fish, and to go to war, and is his sexual partner at night. It is not like here at all. The Marind believe that only an older man may enter the ass of the young. This is so that the sperm will make the boy grow more quickly into a great warrior. There is no sucking of the penis. It is wrong for them to do this, they say."

Nothing in my reading had suggested that any group in New Guinea had ever practiced both fellatio and sodomy. Nor was there a group in which boys and men of the same age had a sexual relationship. The Asmat of the far south appeared to be unique in this. Later, I found out that they were not unique as far as sexual activity between males who were peers is concerned. In 1984, Gilbert Herdt published *Ritualized Homosexuality in Melanesia,* a book of essays by anthropologists about homosexuality within the people they studied, in addition to an introduction that deals with the wide distribution of ritualized homosexuality from New Guinea to Fiji. In the introduction there is a brief section on a society in the Santa Cruz Islands. "It is particularly interesting," Herdt writes, "that two contrary modes of homosexual relations exist side by side in East Bay. The first is *reciprocal* and *egalitarian* sexual satisfaction between peers or friends; each must please the other in return. . . . This type of homosexual contact between peers is apparently rare in Melanesia. . . . The other mode was *asymmetrical* homosexual contact between East Bay men and boys, which is common."

Ronald M. Berndt's *Excess and Restraint* told me of a practice I long wanted to ask about in Asmat. "On another part of this island," I said to Akatpitsjin, "far from here, there are some people called Fore who put a sliver of thorned vine into the hole in the penis and twist it around until blood and semen come out. It is part of the various initiation ceremonies. Is there anything like that here?"

"Oh, no! That is disgusting! Those people are not human!" Akatpitsjin talked this over with the others and all gasped in horror. It took ten minutes before everyone calmed and Akatpitsjin could continue.

"*Mbai*," Akatpitsjin said after he had recovered, "are always friends and always help one another when there is trouble. They are always friends no matter what happens. They remain *mbai* all their lives, until one of them dies. Sometimes one is jealous because his *mbai* has been with another man. He is not jealous when he goes with a woman who is not his wife, only when he is with another man. It is all right to play with another man. He may suck his penis or even enter his ass; that is all right. But he may not have an orgasm. Then, his *mbai* is very angry."

At each of Akatpitsjin's statements, the others nodded their heads in agreement or added slightly different versions of what he was saying. There was no embarassment or holding back. The only problem was in knowing what questions to ask. It astonished me that everything was so open, that everyone knew what went on between Akatpitsjin and myself, that old men listened and talked and young boys, too. Akatpitsjin even called me *mbai* in front of his wife, startling me. Everyone knew what *mbai* did together and there appeared no reason not to discuss all aspects of the relationship. They obviously trusted me completely and even paired off to show me whose *mbai* was whose, allowing me to take photographs. They pointed out the two oldest men of the village, both of whom may have been forty-five. Each had lost his original *mbai*. When both were alone, they adopted one another.

"Yes, Tombias," Akatpitsjin said in answer to a specific question. "There must be balance. There must always be balance between *mbai*. There is no other way. When one *mbai* sucks the penis of his friend, the two may not part until the friend turns around and sucks *his* penis. If one enters the ass of another, the other must turn around and enter *his* ass. *Mbai* must always give back what they take. When I bring fish to the house of Kayet, my *mbai*, he will bring me sago the next time he goes into the jungle. When I bring him sago, he will later bring me fish or sago worms. When I am angry at someone in Pirimapun, Kayet must come with me to fight him. When Kayet has a fight, I must help him. We must share what we have. Everything must remain in balance."

Reciprocity and balance, I knew, was the way of life throughout Asmat. It touched on all close relationships in a manner very complex. My problem in Buepis in not sharing the last of the tobacco arose from this principle. The men considered that I had the magical means of obtaining anything I wanted and therefore needed nothing from them in exchange. They expected me to share everything.

I had at that time been writing regularly to Dr. Rhoda Metraux. When she learned of the need for balance in the sexual relationships between men, she encouraged me to obtain as much information as possible, not only about sexual activity but about the reciprocity that kept the universe as well as daily life symmetrical and calm. A constant flow of semen was obligatory in times of strife to ward off dangers that threatened the cosmos and was a requisite in equalizing the powers of the ancestors with that of their living relations. Akatpitsjin suggested that equilibrium was necessary not only between men, but between men and women as well, for it was the vagina that acted as a counterbalance to the penis.

"And what about your wives?" I asked Akatpitsjin. "Do they know of your sexual relationship with your *mbai*? Don't they get jealous?"

The men slapped one another's shoulders and recalled having had many experiences with women other than their wives. Everyone fooled his wife sometimes and the men were proud and talked about it at length.

"Our women know everything and do not get jealous. Only

when we are with another woman do they get angry. They get very angry then, but not when we are with our *mbai.*

"We sometimes do have other women. Our wives beat us with firewood when they find out, but we are very careful to keep them from finding out.

"We get angry with our wives too. Sometimes they go with other men and try to hide this, but we men are smarter and know what is happening. We beat them and sometimes throw them out. We make them go back to their father's house if they have many sexual affairs with other men. We do not let them come back. We take another wife, a new, young one."

"If you don't like your *mbai* or fight with him too much, can you change to another man?"

"Oh, no! It is different with our *mbai.* Maybe we get angry with him, but our *mbai* is our *mbai* until one of us dies. We cannot throw him out like a wife. We do not want to. He is with us all our life."

"What happens," I asked, "if you catch your wife having sex with another man?"

"Oh! I beat her up," answered Akatpitsjin.

"What happens if you catch your *mbai* with another man?"

"Oh! I beat up the other man!"

"You don't beat your *mbai?*"

"Oh, no! I never beat him. He is my *mbai!*"

Akatpitsjin never failed to surprise and amuse me.

"What about such villages as Buepis and Basim? Do they also have *mbai* friendships?"

"Yes. They do, but they are changing now."

"What other villages have it?"

"Many villages. All the villages up and down the Casuarina Coast. The *mbai* start down at Pirimapun, in that area, maybe even farther, and then they go up to Omandesep and Jow."

"How do you know this?"

"Because some men used to have their *mbai* in other villages. When there was *papisj* in the past, sometimes it was necessary to travel long distances, to Otsjenep, to Jow. Then we would stay several days for a feast because it was such a long trip and we could not come back in one day."

I could discover no words or attitudes concerning the active or passive roles in the sexual life of the people in my village. However, I later learned from a young man from Jamasj who worked in the museum in Agats that in the northwest *ndu fa tetame* literally means "I give ass" and *ndo tsjemen afa towai* is "I give my penis into the ass." The young man insisted that he had never participated in any sexual activity that involved another man, a statement I believed; by the time he was born, sexual relations between men had already been forbidden in his area by missionaries and the government.

Since sexual intercourse in *mbai* relationships appears always to be reciprocal in the south, there is no need for specific words. The single role, in fact, may not exist as it does in Western societies where, until recently, participants in sodomy and fellation usually take only one role. The passive role is considered feminine, the active masculine. Such considerations are not part of Asmat thought processes. The only possible exceptions are those rare men called *cemenopok,* no-penis, who grow up with a penis so small the women will have nothing to do with them. It is said that every village has at least one *cemenopok* and that he unashamedly plays the passive role with other men.*

"What about women having sex together?" I asked one day.

"What do you mean?"

"You know. I mean women playing with one another sexually."

Akatpitsjin burst into laughter. He explained to the others and every one laughed. The men and boys grabbed at one another's crotches. They hugged one another and pressed their bodies together. They rolled on the floor; they jumped up and down. They held their bellies, sat up, lay down, rolled back and forth.

---

*I do not know whether this is the condition known as micropenis, which is sometimes due to a deficiency of testosterone, for I never saw one. The men describe this type of penis in erection as less than the size of their smallest finger.

"But why would they want to play with each other?"

"For the same reason they play with men, to have pleasure."

"But that's impossible with another woman!"

Everyone laughed again, trying to visualize two women having sexual intercourse. They denied any such possiblity. I never got a proper answer to this since I was never able to question the women themselves on the subject. Boelaars, however, writes, about neighbors of the Asmat, the Jaqai, that "Homosexuality . . . is not uncommon among both sexes." He says nothing further about females.

Akatpitsjin, of course, was my main informant. Every day, when it wasn't raining, we walked along the edge of the Arafura Sea at low tide. We could smell the salt in its waters. Akatpitsjin surprised me one morning by saying, "Everything is in change now. Sometimes it is good. Sometimes, I do not understand what is happening. We are happy that you are here. We like you and you are like my *mbai*. And you bring us tobacco and metal and we taste strange foods. We have clothing and we are Catholic now. We are happy, and like to keep you here.

"We understand you better than we understand the ways of Pastor. You are like one of us. You do not get angry when we tell you what we do. You are with us. But you and Pastor both have good things and we want them, too. Our ancestors are angry with us now. We no longer follow the old ways and we no longer listen to them. Pastor comes and teaches us new ideas that make our ancestors unhappy. We do not avenge their deaths like we used to. We do not listen to them. They are angry and maybe the spirits will stop the sago from growing. Maybe there will be no more fish in the rivers around us.

"We no longer have warfare where many men are killed. We go to Pastor when we are hurting and when we are sick and when we are shaking with malaria. And now we have more men and women and more children in the village.

"Still, the young are not content here. They are no longer interested in learning to sing the old songs. They want guitars and they want to sing and dance in another way. They do not want to learn how to carve the figures of our ancestors. They want to carve to make money quickly, but they do not want to learn *how* to carve. It is enough that they make poor carvings that they paint and take to Agats to sell.

"Only old men like me carve drums now. Only the old men go into the men's house. Only old men play the drums and sing the old songs and tell the old stories. The young want to go to Merauke and to Sorong and they stay with other Asmat there. They do not earn money. They do not work. They go there thinking they will bring back money and gifts, but they return with nothing. They have been to Merauke but they are not important men like the men who have taken heads or the men who are real carvers. They are nothing."

By this time, we had returned to the village and were walking along the bank of the narrow stream. Mangrove trees arched across from both sides and tangled together. A wave of sweetness filled the air, floating downstream with the current.

Chapter

TWENTY

I dreamed that night of another world, one in which I am running through the forest, no jungle growth around me but leafless trees, the sun behind the bare branches dazzling me. I feel myself there; I feel spirits everywhere around me, among the trees, within the lakes, inside the rooms of all the houses, benevolent spirits filling the rooms with the aura of those who had lived there, ancestral spirits of long ago. I see myself running in the early morning, past West House, still without a single light, turning left into the stands of pine and birch, hemlocks, beech and oak. Patches of snow glisten as my boots splash shallow pools of melted ice and crackle the glazed earth. The Whitney estate, seen clearly in wintertime, its stables empty, looks lonely as a Hopper house, the jockeys and horses gone to warmer climes, the track a ghostly Ryder. The thumping sounds of pumping water disturb the would-be silence, though there are, too, the calls of pileated woodpeckers and blue jays. I pass the first of four lakes and turn to the right toward the stone tower and, once there, turn left to continue past Lake Christina. Finally, I reach the entrance road, go right, look over at Lake Alan on my left, and run slowly uphill, the way curving up to the great lawn and on past the mansion.

It is all clear in my dream and conforms with reality. The run is my daily exercise, a mile around the lakes. I stop to catch my breath, then climb the stairs at the end of the building that houses the garage and offices. I enter the kitchen where Nellie, chief cook, smiles and invites me in for coffee. She is putting together the dinner meal, macaroni on meatless Thursdays. Susan, second cook, big, black, cheerful, and Sylvia, small and stocky, her dyed black

201

hair in wisps at the sides of her face, are making piles of sand-wiches for the twelve guests. They pack the slices of wheat and rye and white with freshly roasted sago worms that drip fat through their working fingers. The lunch pails already have their carrot sticks and cookies. I am with the tribe of Yaddo, my hosts prepar-ing food for a feast.

Akatpitsjin appears at the doorway, naked, paddle in hand. He props it against a wall, enters the small dining room and sits at the head of the table. "Poached crocodile eggs," he tells Beverly, the waitress. Other guests appear. I sit at Akatpitsjin's right and, al-though he is thirty-five years my junior, he is my father. I am suddenly in his lap and he cuddles me. The other guests, male and female, are part of our family, my siblings. I shrink and disappear into Akatpitsjin, as if moving into a male womb. Guests are dis-cussing Janet Frame, whose work they have not read. Their lan-guage is gobbledegook and I understand nothing. I am at my place again at table. Janet is now at Akatpitsjin's left, her fuzzy hair a halo around her head. She looks at Akatpitsjin, then looks at me. "You are having an affair," she whispers in her tiny voice. "I want to join you."

Akatpitsjin takes his napkin in hand, pats his lips and says ex-actly what he had said earlier that day, exactly what is down in my journal. "Of course there is sex between three people." He speaks with a clipped British accent. He wears a necklace of job's tear seeds and cassowary quills, its centerpiece a human atlas bone, the first vertebra of the neck. The guests listen intently to him. A friend enters and sits next to me, after he kisses Janet on the cheek. He is silent, tongue-tied in front of his idol, Miss Frame. He smiles at me, touches my arm, climbs onto the table, stretches, bends, and does a grand jeté elancé, landing in Janet's lap. She cuddles him. Akatpitsjin has been talking and we all listen. "Ev-erything is in change now," he continues. "We are forgetting the ways of our ancestors." He gets up, lift his bows and arrows and shoots all the guests but Janet, my friend, and myself. The bodies separate into pieces and, after they are cooked, we eat them. I hold up a piece of flesh and say, "Here is Georgina, a painter of renown.

I am eating her and will have her talent." Later, after I have chewed and swallowed Georgina's cheek, I pick up another piece of meat and say, "This is the hand of Paul. He was a fine writer. Now I too will be a good writer."

I am floating vertically, my feet straight up, my head down. I am descending like a missile, speeding downward into a forest of thorned sago. I am terrified. I wake up, my body covered with perspiration. I am back in my village, in the teacher's house where I am confused for a moment. My eyes make out the form of Akatpitsjin lying next to me. We get up and put on our shorts. After a breakfast of wild chicken eggs and coffee, Akatpitsjin repeats what he had said the day before and what he had said in my dream.

"Of course there is sex between three people. It happens often." But it turned out that one of the three is always an onlooker rather than a participant. This is true even when a man is with his two wives or when he is with his wife and his *mbai*. "These things are in change now, and we are forgetting the ways of our ancestors. The soldiers come now and take our women and sometimes one soldier will want two. We do not like what they are doing but they have guns and we can do nothing."

"Tell me, Akatpitsjin," I said, going back to another conversation. "Pastor comes to the village and you go to church. You are Catholic now. Not long ago, I know, you were all baptized, everyone in the village. You go to confession and tell him all your sins. Do you tell him everything? What about what happens between you and your *mbai*? What about me? Do you speak about this at all? You say he knows nothing of what happens between men. How is this possible?" It was odd to me that sex between men could still be going on when Father Pietre was so violently anti-homosexual.

"Pastor knows nothing. It is forbidden to say anything of this to him. Everyone knows that nothing must be said and no one says anything. We confess that we have had five women or seven women who are not our wives. We confess this and other things too, but we say nothing of the relationship with our *mbai*. It is forbidden. Pastor listens carefully and tells us what to do about our sins but he hears nothing of our *mbai*.

"What would happen if you did confess this?"

"Oh, Pastor would stop it, like he has stopped *papisj*. Pastor has already said that sex between men is sinful and that the government too has forbidden it."

Additional information on the sexual life came out slowly over the next week, since as always I was gathering material on design and on tools and weapons as well. Often the subject of sex was brought up by others. The talk was never limited to any age group; everyone talked, old men, young men, children. Everyone had something to say. In a group there was barely enough time for me to look up from my journal to see who was speaking, it all came out so rapidly, so easily. Children chattered about their own sex lives, telling how they played together with boys and girls when bathing in the streams. Young men and old cleverly acted out sexual scenes in a kind of sign language or with their bodies as if they were playing charades. Akatpitsjin became moderator and translator, repeating everything carefully to make sure the information I was putting down was correct.

"There are times," said one of the men, "when I am alone in the jungle and there is no one around, no *mbai,* no woman, and the terrible urge comes over me to have intercourse. But no one is there. What is there to do? I make a small hole in the mud and lie face down. I put my penis in the hole and wiggle my hips and rub myself in the mud. It is very good."

"We are not like the Marind, here," said the oldest man, who knew a great deal even though he had never been out of Asmat. "We do not separate the boys from the girls before initiation. They play together, like the boys play together. They examine one another's genitals and insert a finger into a vagina or anus and sometimes a penis enters the girls. We do not stop this kind of play."

Attitudes vary from culture to culture in New Guinea, although each is sometimes offended by its neighbor's contrary practices. Every group has its patterns of behavior that are considered proper and patterns that are considered abnormal. I was lucky to have found Akatpitsjin, for he made me go as far as I could in what my early life had insisted was unnatural. With him I fitted into a pattern of life that was completely acceptable. It is not that I had ever felt myself to be abnormal, only that I appeared so in the minds of others. However, at the same time that I realized that I could go no further in my search, I discovered that I was satisfied with myself, with who I was. I felt part of a family that was part of all families.

I can see now that my time in Asmat was an initiation. In fact, I have been going through various stages of initiation throughout my life, without ever having been aware of it. What were Mexico and Peru but steps along the way? In Asmat itself, the first steps were surely the ritual suckling of the extensions of my body, when I was nourishing others and others were nourishing me. The men could not have known that they were involved in a sequence of events that would lead me into revelations about myself, but they were part of them. Several of the men were close to me and were certainly family, but it is in the progression of my relations with Akatpitsjin that the other steps might be seen clearly. It was he who was the instigator, the one who moved me to new levels. It was he who induced me into adulthood, as if he were my mother's brother, my father. It was he who announced to one and all that I was his *mbai,* that I was related to him, as all others had such relations. It was he who provoked me into a new world by saying, "I must balance," and it was he who completed my initiation by taking me to his wife, even though I failed and he consummated the act in my place. His understanding and consciousness of my dilemma gave me a sense of security and wholeness that I had never felt before. Later, much later, I recognized that I was satiated, full of Asmat, full of New Guinea, ready to return to New York.

When I was packed, Akatpitsjin carried my patrol box on his shoulder, his free hand holding onto my elbow. He was smiling as if I were arriving instead of leaving. His eyes glistened. All five of his children clustered around him. Other men, all of them of the village, it seemed, and some women, stood at the bank of the river. The canoe that had come from Basim was banked in the mud.

Five paddlers stood there and greeted me with arms waving and shouts of my name. Akatpitsjin waved to them, too, showing off his new wristwatch. My goods were quickly loaded and I stepped into the canoe with the paddle Akatpitsjin had given me. By then I was able to stand and balance myself properly in the dugout. Akatpitsjin and the children pushed the canoe into the water shouting, *"Nder momo! Nder momo!"* I shouted back, and my paddlers moved us downstream toward the open sea.

Glossary of Asmat (A)
and Indonesian (I) Words

(I) *Ada*—there is
(I) *Aduh*—alas! Oh! dear me! Ah!
(A) *Ainor*—mysterious and frightening design on shields of south Asmat
(A) *Akat, akato*—good, wonderful
(A) *Ata*—to want
(A) *Atakam*—to speak
(I) *Babi*—pig
(I) *Balas*—balance
(I) *Bapak*—father, elder man, sir; term of address
(A) *Basu suangkus*—ritual carving in certain villages, translated as: the making visible of the heads of men who have been killed in battle; literally: visible killed heads
(I) *Biawak*—lizard
(A) *Bipane*—shell nosepiece; also, the design
(I) *Camat*—local head of the government throughout Indonesia; roughly equivalent to an assistant district officer
(A) *Cemen, tsjemen, tamen*—penis
(A) *Cemenopok*—name given to men with very small penes; literally: no penis
(A) *Dasan*—afraid
(A) *Djemes, jemesj, jamas*—shield
(A) *Djimatsj*—heterosexual intercourse
(A) *Dje, dze, jew, jeu*—men's house, feast house
(A) *Eu*—crocodile
(A) *Fa*—buttocks, anus
(A) *Faper*—sodomy
(A) *Faper ameris*—reciprocal sodomy
(A) *Faper (feper) mbimar*—to enter the anus
(A) *Far*—butterfly

(*I*)   *Hurahura*—an uproar
(*I*)   *Hutan*—jungle
(*A*)   *Imu-mu*—a ritual relationship between a man and a boy
(*A*)   *Ipitsj*—man
(*A*)   *Isap*—smoke, cigarette
(*I*)   *Kali*—river
(*A*)   *Kom*—a small, crispy fruit
(*I*)   *Mau*—to want
(*A*)   *Mbai*—a ritual relationship between two men of approximately the
          same age
(*A*)   *Mbi*—water
(*A*)   *Mbi urum*—a ritual of friendship and adoption
(*A*)   *Ndat*—spirit
(*A*)   *Ndatipitsj*—spirit man
(*A*)   *Ndei, ndein*—come, to come
(*A*)   *Nder momo*—a greeting, used most often with foreigners; Hello,
          goodbye; literally: I love you
(*A*)   *Ndo fa tetame*—I give ass; to be the passive partner in sodomy
(*A*)   *Ndo tsjemen afai towai*—I give my penis into the ass; to be the
          active partner in sodomy
(*A*)   *Ndoram ata yima*—I want balance
(*A*)   *O*—pig
(*A*)   *Omen*—the sound of grunting
(*A*)   *Omu*—a ritual carving of northwest Asmat
(*A*)   *Opok*—no, nothing
(*I*)   *Orang*—man
(*I*)   *Orang hutan*—jungle man—often used in a derogatory way
(*A*)   *Papisj*—wife exchange
(*I*)   *Parang*—bush knife, machete
(*A*)   *Per*—to hook together
(*I*)   *Rumah*—house
(*I*)   *Rumah sakit*—hospital
(*I*)   *Rupiah*—unit of currency in Indonesia
(*I*)   *Rupiah tidak ada*—there is no money
(*I*)   *Sakit*—illness
(*I*)   *Salamat jalan*—goodbye, have a good trip (said to the person
          leaving)
(*I*)   *Salamat tinggal*—goodbye, stay well (said to the person staying)
(*A*)   *Sasor*—a kind of crab

(*I*)   *Saya*—I

(*I*)   *Saya mau balas*—I want balance, I want to balance

(*A*)   *Sini*—no, not

(*A*)   *Sini dasan*—do not be afraid

(*A*)   *Tamen mbe mbakuman*—to suck a man's penis

(*A*)   *Tamen mbai sumapun*—to enter the anus of a man's ritual friend

(*A*)   *Tar*—flying fox

(*A*)   *Tare*—former times

(*A*)   *Tare atakam*—in olden times, to speak of olden times

(*A*)   *Tarep*—flying fox feet

(*A*)   *Tempe* —carved housepost in northwest Asmat

(*I*)   *Tidak*—no, not

(*A*)   *Yipit a minau tamen emefafarimis*—to peel back the foreskin of one's penis; to masturbate

Bibliography

Berndt, Ronald M. *Excess and Restraint*. Chicago: University of Chicago Press, 1961.

Gajdusek, D. Carleton. "Physiological and Psychological Characteristics of Stone Age Man," *Engineering and Science*, Volume 33, Number 6, April 1970.

Herdt, Gilbert. *Guardians of the Flutes*. New York: McGraw-Hill Book Co. 1981.

Herdt, Gilbert, ed. *Ritualized Homosexuality in Melanesia*. Berkeley: University of California Press, 1984.

Van Baal, J. *Dema*. The Hague: Martinus Nijhoff, 1966.

Zegwaard, G. "Headhunting Practices of Netherlands New Guinea," in *American Anthropologist*, 1959, Volume 61, pp. 1020-1041.

211